CROKE PARK

A HISTORY

TIM CAREY is a former curator of the GAA Museum, Croke Park.
A graduate of Trinity College Dublin, he has written two other books
Mountjoy – The Story of a Prison (Cork, 2000) and *Hanged for Ireland*
(Dublin, 2001) and co-authored *The Martello Towers of Dublin*
(Dublin, 2012). He lives in Dublin, where he is currently Heritage Officer
with Dún Laoghaire-Rathdown County Council.

The 1954 All-Ireland football final between Meath and Kerry.

TIM CAREY

CROKE PARK

A HISTORY

The Collins Press

First published in hardback in 2004 by

The Collins Press,

West Link Park,

Doughcloyne,

Wilton,

Cork

First published in paperback in 2007

This updated paperback published 2013

British Library Cataloguing in Publication data.

Carey, Tim

Croke Park, A History - Updated ed.

1. Croke Park (Dublin, Ireland) - History

2. Gaelic Athletic Association - History

3. Gaelic games - Ireland - History

I. Title 796'.068'415

ISBN-13: 9781848891722

Printed in Malta by Gutenberg Press Limited

Cover design by Anú Design, Tara

Typeset by Burns Design

Cover photographs

Front, top: 3 February 2007; the Artane Band lead the Dublin and Tyrone football teams during
the parade before the start of the league game (courtesy David Maher/Sportsfile www.sportsfile.com);

bottom: 17 September 2006; All-Ireland final day, the Sam Maguire displays the colours of
Mayo and Kerry (courtesy Brendan Moran/Sportsfile www.sportsfile.com);

Back: 1980 All-Ireland hurling final between Galway and Limerick
(courtesy Connelly Collection/Sportsfile www.sportsfile.com).

Contents

ACKNOWLEDGEMENTS

As with any work of this kind there are a number of people and organisations that have made it possible. Firstly, I would like to thank the GAA for supporting this publication. I am honoured to have had the privilege of writing a history of our most important sports stadium. I would also like to thank Coca-Cola Bottlers Ireland (CCBI) for their kind sponsorship of this publication. I would also like to express my gratitude to Dún Laoghaire-Rathdown County Council for being supportive during the writing of this book.

There are a number of people to whom I am personally grateful. I am indeed indebted to Micheál Ó Muircheartaigh for kindly and generously compiling a variety of people's reminiscences that appear throughout the book. I owe a huge amount to Marcus de Búrca for proofing the manuscript and setting me straight a few times. Of course, any errors, omissions or mistakes are unfortunately my own. Many thanks to Ray McManus and Sportsfile for permitting the reproduction of a number of their superb pictures in this book. I would also like to thank the staff of the GAA Museum for their support – Tony McGuinness, Maria Gorman, Eoin O'Driscoll, Barry Shiels and Joanne Clarke but in particular I am grateful to Deirdre Flood for all her help. A sincere thanks is also due to Pat for his input into this book. I would like to thank Cara Ronan for assisting with some of the research. The members of staff of the National Library of Ireland Reading Room and Photographic Archive were, as usual, at all times courteous and helpful during the course of the research. Thanks also to Irene Duncan, Anne Gallagher, Des McMahon and Gilroy McMahon Architects, Chris Gogarty of Seamus Monahan and Partners, Donncha O'Dulaing, Fergal McGill, Paul Turnell, Independent Newspapers, Gaelic Art, Larry Ryder and the Hibernian Athletic Historical Association.

I would like to express my deepest gratitude to my wife Sinéad for making this book possible and our children Jennifer and Aaron for their patience with their father who was writing this book when he should have been spending time with them.

PICTURE CREDITS

Courtesy GAA Museum and Archive pages ii–iii, 2 (all), 6 (top), 7, 11, 15, 20, 21, 22 (all), 26–27, 28, 31, 34–35, 38, 43, 51, 61, 62, 64 (bottom), 66–67, 68–69, 71, 74, 77, 78, 79, 80, 82, 83, 85, 89, 96 (both), 99, 101, 104, 108, 110–111, 114 (both), 116 (top), 117 (top), 116–117 (bottom), 119, 120, 124, 127 (insert), 131 (both), 132 (insert), 133, 135 (bottom), 138–139, 142, 156, 159, 163.

Courtesy Artane Band pages 75, 112.

Courtesy Anne Gallagher page 92.

Courtesy National Library of Ireland pages 52–53, 54, 63, 64 (top).

Courtesy G.A. Duncan pages 6 (second from top), 112 (both), 141.

Courtesy Connolly Collection (Sportsfile – www.sportfile.com) pages 88, 132 (main),135 (top), 144–145.

Courtesy Colman Doyle page 143.

Courtesy Sportsfile (www.sportsfile.com) pages ii–iii, 6 (bottom), 149, 151, 152, 167 (both), 173, 176–177, 179 (both), 182.

Courtesy Hibernian Athletics Historical Association pages 29, 72–73.

Courtesy Independent Newspapers pages 6 (second from bottom), 42, 93, 97, 115, 123, 125, 127.

Courtesy Gaelic Art pages 90–91.

Courtesy Gilroy McMahon pages 172–173.

RTÉ Archives pages 37, 41, 59.

COLOUR SECTION

Courtesy GAA Museum pages 1–6, 7 (bottom left and right), 8 (top left and right), 9 (bottom).

Courtesy Sportsfile (www.sportsfile.com) pages 7 (top), 8 (bottom), 9 (top), 10–14, 16.

Courtesy Maxwell's Dublin page 15.

A view of the new Croke Park.

Introduction

The first time I went to Croke Park was to see the Dublin-Galway football final in 1983. Coincidentally, it was this match which would ultimately lead to the redevelopment of the stadium, which in turn led to the production of this book. The first thoughts I had of writing this book came almost as soon as I began working in the GAA Museum in Croke Park. It was early 2001 and the stadium was in the middle of construction. It was also in the middle of the controversy about opening the stadium to other sports. At the end of a day's work in the Museum I would go home to see Croke Park on television, as all sides of the debate were aired. The media coverage of this episode brought Croke Park out from the confines of the sports bulletin into the main headlines. It seemed amazing to me that there was not a history written of such a unique and important place as Croke Park.

Croke Park is not just a sporting venue. The single most important asset of the GAA, it has been a reflection of the strength of the organisation as well as an influence on it. At the same time, Croke Park has been a salient feature of Irish life. The first Gaelic games were played at what was then the City and Suburban Sports Ground in the 1890s but it was not until the first decade of the twentieth century that Croke Park became the Gaelic Athletic Association's most important venue. Since then it has evolved through various phases until its most recent and magnificent reconstruction.

Writing a history of such an iconic place as Croke Park is a daunting prospect. The complete history of the stadium is truly an epic story. Since Gaelic games were first played at the Jones' Road venue many thousands of players have played there, while millions have watched from behind ropes, on grassy banks, on rickety stands and in the spectacular setting of the coliseum of today. Obviously, for a book to attempt to document everything that has happened in Croke Park would make it far too long to be practical – it would run to many volumes, most of which would not be relevant to the vast majority of readers.

This book is not a history of everything that has happened in Croke Park. It concentrates on what I see as the most important of the main events, personalities, key matches and trends that have influenced Croke Park. Unfortunately, this means that most of us who have been influenced by Croke Park, but who have failed to affect it in turn, do not feature in this book. The reality is that Croke Park may have been important to us but we have not been important to it. I have tried to address this issue and to convey some idea of the influence that Croke Park has exerted over the lives of countless individuals by interspersing throughout the book short personal reminiscences from a wide variety of people. They are the mere tip of a very large iceberg.

Croke Park Timeline

1884	GAA founded
1891	Parnellite split reflected in the ranks of the GAA
1891	10 September, first GAA athletics meeting at Jones' Road
1896	21 March, first Gaelic game at Jones' Road
1901	Jim Nowlan elected President of GAA and Luke O'Toole appointed secretary
1902	Archbishop Croke dies
1903	2 August, London win All-Ireland at Jones' Road
1908	Frank Dineen buys Jones' Road
1913	Croke Memorial tournament held which raised funds to purchase Jones' Road
1913	October, GAA decides to purchase Jones' Road
1913	22 December, GAA takes ownership of Jones' Road, now Croke Park
1916	Frank Dineen dies
1917	October, Irish Volunteers Convention held at Croke Park
1919	Croke Park management committee established
1920	21 November, Bloody Sunday at Croke Park
1923	4 March, Liam MacCarthy Cup presented for first time
1923	June, Croke Park Fête
1924	August, First *Tailteann* Games held
1924	August, Rodeo held at Croke Park
1925	First scoreboard at Croke Park
1926	'The Soldier's Song' played for the first time before the start of match at Croke Park
1926	17 March, Hogan Stand officially named in honour of Michael Hogan
1926	September, Otto Pelzer sets world record for 1500m at Croke Park
1926	August, Croke Park provides first radio broadcast of a field game in Europe

1928 Second *Tailteann* Games held at Croke Park

1931 Cork and Kilkenny meet three times to decide All-Ireland hurling championship

1932 Third *Tailteann* Games held at Croke Park

1934 GAA Golden Jubilee

1938 21 August, Cusack Stand officially opened. First broadcast by Micheál O'Hehir from Croke Park

1939 3 September, Thunder and Lightning Final

1944 Cork hurlers win fourth All-Ireland in a row

1947 All-Ireland football final played in New York

1950 Canal End Terrace opens

1952 Nally Stand opens

1953 American football match in aid of the Red Cross played at Croke Park

1954 September, record crowd of 84,856 watch Cork and Wexford in hurling final

1956 Pageant of Cuchulann held at Croke Park

1959 7 June, new Hogan Stand officially opened

1961 Patrician Year Mass held at Croke Park

1961 Record crowd of 90,556 at Croke Park for Down v Offally All-Ireland football final

1962 6 August, Telefís Éireann broadcast first live television game from Croke Park

1966 Events commemorating fiftieth Anniversary of 1916 Rising held at Croke Park

1970 World handball championship held in Croke Park

1971 McNamee Commission reports on many aspects of the GAA including Croke Park

1972 19 July, Muhammad Ali fights at Croke Park

1973 Willwood Games at Croke Park

1983 Events at Dublin v Galway All-Ireland football final prompt reconstruction of Hill 16 which then leads to complete redevelopment of ground

1984 GAA Centenary year

1984 First series of games of International Rules at Croke Park

1985 U2 play sell-out concert at Croke Park

1988 Hill 16 reconstructed

1990 Master Plan for Croke Park completed

1992 2 February, initial application for Planning Persmission of new Croke Park lodged with Dublin Corporation

1993 9 March, planning permission for Croke Park redevelopment granted

1993 September, beginning of demolition of Cusack Stand

1996 Premium level of Cusack Stand opened

1998 GAA Museum opened

1998 Canal End demolished

1999 October, Hogan Stand demolished

2001 April, GAA Congress votes against opening Croke Park to other games

2002 Pitch at Croke Park re-laid

2002 New Hogan Stand opened

2003 June-July, Opening and closing ceremonies of Special Olympics held at Croke Park

2005 April, GAA Congress votes in favour of opening Croke Park to other games

2007 3 February, Dublin v Tyrone is first match played under floodlights at Croke Park

2007 11 and 24 February, Irish rugby team play France and England at Croke Park

2007 24 and 28 March, Irish soccer team play Wales and Slovakia at Croke Park

2009 31 January, GAA125 anniversary celebrations start at Croke Park

2009 April, Croke Park awarded RIAI Gold Medal, the premier award for architecture in Ireland

2009 24–27 July, U2 play three sell-out concerts

2010 June, Croke Park Agreement signed

2011 18 May, Queen Elizabeth II visits Croke Park

2012 6 June, Olympic Torch at Croke Park

2013 22 December, Croke Park is 100 years old

CHAPTER ONE

1896–1913

1903 football final between Kerry and Kildare.

Broadcaster Brendán O'Hehir finished his autobiography, *Over the Bar*, with the story of Billy Doonan. Doonan was from Cavan and during the Second World War he joined the Irish Army and trained as a radio operator. Dissatisfied at the lack of action, he left and crossed the border into Northern Ireland to join the British Army, becoming a radio operator. In 1943 he was part of the invasion force during the Italian campaign. One Sunday in September he went missing. A search party was sent out for him and he was found up a tree on a steep hillside with his radio listening to Micheál O'Hehir's commentary of the All-Ireland football final between Cavan and Roscommon at Croke Park.[1]

Most Irish people, and certainly those with any interest in Gaelic Games, can identify with this story. Croke Park, or 'Croker', is central to the Irish psyche. The trip to Croke Park is a well-rehearsed pilgrimage for many people. For those who go to Croke Park on a regular basis they often have a routine for the day, with a well-worn path along favoured routes. For people from counties like Tipperary, Cork, Kilkenny, Kerry, Galway or Dublin there are little known short-cuts, a regular train carriage, meeting points, places where one is assured of getting a good feed, the familiar pub, a usual place on the Hill, the Hogan, the Cusack. For those from the so-called 'weaker' counties the achievement of going to the headquarters of the GAA is an event that is anticipated with a yearning desire. For everyone, the day is both an intensely personal experience lived privately in one's own thoughts and one that is inextricably linked to the communal. Towns, villages, counties on the move. A comparison has often been made between sport and religion. The parallels are many. But in this modern religion the stadiums are the cathedrals. There are no pews, altars or stained-glass windows but stands, terraces, open skies and a field of green.

The first article to outline, from an individual's point of view, the collective experience at what is now Croke Park was published in the *Gaelic News* of July 1897. On this occasion it was the meeting of Dublin's Young Irelands and Arravale Rovers of Tipperary in the Dr Croke Cup football final. The article is from another time. What we know as Croke Park was the City and Suburban Sports Grounds at Jones' Road, usually known as simply Jones' Road, which was rented by the GAA for some of its fixtures. It was first used for a GAA event on 10 September 1892 when an athletics meeting was held there. The first important Gaelic games match at Jones' Road took place just a year before the article was written, when a Leinster football final was played there on 1 March 1896 between O'Mahonys of Meath and Isles of the Seas from Dublin. Despite the obvious passage of time evident in the article there is also a timelessness to the atmosphere and the emotions of the big match experience:

All bets on bad weather being called off at dawn, and if we failed to discern the sun coming over those eastern hilltops and a heavy, murky atmosphere precluded a sky of blue, still the day ripened out into a proverbial summer's one, rather oppressive to the players, but delightful from a spectator's point of view. Long before the scheduled time for starting streams of spectators were seen wending their way toward's Jones's Road. Among them you had the proverbial Gaelic man, the clerk, the artizan, and now and again an outsider flashed past heavily weighted by a contingent of Navan Mahonys or Crom-a-Boos. In the midst of all you had a *paterfamilias,* the central figure of a batch of sons whom circumstances prevented from being born in Tipperary soil, they listened attentively as the old man recounted the former deeds of the "matchless men", and now he was taking them to see the grandest teams that ever played for his native county, he was taking the youngsters to see the sons of the old sod win. Tipperary women, resident in Dublin, were also among the throng, whilst international Rugby and members of nearly every walk of life helped to swell the vast crowds.

It was a day of early bed-leaving and many a Gael emulated the proverbial lark. For some reason or other flying visits were paid and repaid to the entrance to the grounds, whilst hundreds congregated on the Canal Bridge awaiting the arrival of the teams. At 11:30 a cheer announced the arrival of George Roche, the homely-looking full-back of the Irelands, forming the head of a flying wedge of admirers, his actions and ways being hung upon by a dozen football worshippers.

As time drew near the crowd anxiously scanned those long streets for the advent of the Tipperary Team. At last the prolonged rattle of wheels came faintly on the breeze, and suddenly the "outsiders" appeared in view, the sunburnt athletic sons of Tipperary jumping off the cars with the confidence begotten of superb health and manhood. A few had their amber and black jerseys tucked tidily under their arms, and all bore the unmistakable traits of the athlete. Jauntily they strode down to the grounds, as did the hitherto unbeaten champions …

By 12 o'clock the entrances to the arena were besieged, and the turnstiles played their merry tune of click, click, click. The clamour was loud and the assault heavy, the anxious Gaels, armed with the talismanic pasteboard daubing over each other's shoulders to get into the grounds. In a short time the side walks of the neighbouring streets, lately so thick with people, were deserted, all the lines of men seen moving towards the arena for hours previously having taken up positions on the field. A tedious, long wait followed through the proverbial photographing of the teams, but at last the vivid green jersies (sic) of the Irelands headed by Kelly, Hession, and Roche, came into view, and a ringing cheer greeted the champions, to be repeated later on in greater volume when every man "exiled" from the rolling plains of gallant Tipperary sent up a shout for the famous Rovers, headed by the two Quaynes [Quanes] and McInerney, in the old Clanwilliam colours of black and amber bars. The spin of the coin went in favour of Tipperary, who taking counsel with "Billy" Quayne [Quane], elected to play from the Clonliffe goal. As the men clasped hands fully 7,000 spectators were on the grounds, and when the last buzz of excitement dwindled down until each one held his breath, a shrill blow of Mr Lyons' whistle announced the advent of the fray, in goes the leather, and the spectators giving vent to their pent-up feelings, a roar awoke the surrounding echoes, which never ceased through-out the hour.[2]

When this article was written the GAA was just thirteen years old. Today there are over 2,000 clubs in Ireland (not to mention those abroad) and attendance figures alone for championship games at Croke Park are well over 1,000,000 annually. However, what is now the largest sporting and cultural organisation in Ireland went through a very difficult and painful period after its foundation in 1884. Indeed, to say that it faced difficulties is an understatement. The finances of the association were in a critical condition. The amateur association was incurring mounting debts and at one point the winding up of the association was proposed. Compounding the financial problems, and partly a cause of it, were political divides in the association. For an organisation founded with explicit political overtones – to roll back English influence in Ireland and assert a vision of an Irish Ireland – and one that had the potential to exert huge influence over young men, it was inevitable that the outside political world would

SUPPLEMENT TO THE GAELIC NEWS, JULY, 1897.

Souvenir of Dr. Croke Cup Football Final, Jones's Road, Sunday, June 13th, 1897.

DUBLIN YOUNG IRELAND FOOTBALL TEAM.

J. Mahony. J. Heslin. — Gannon.
S. Mooney. E. Hessian. A. Graham. R. Flood. — Brady. J. Teeling. J. Ledwidge.
P. Heslin. R. Curtis. M. Byrne. L. O'Kelly. J. Kennedy. M. Hayes. G. Roche. T. Errity.

TIPPERARY (ARRAVALE) ROVERS FOOTBALL TEAM

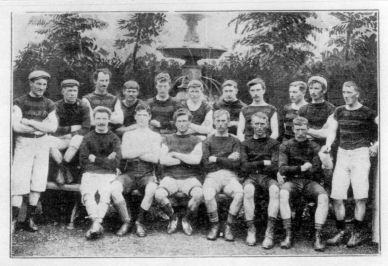

R. Quane. M. McInerney. P. Glasheen. R. Swords. W. Shea. M. Connor. W. J. Ryan. P. Dwyer. J. Carew. M. Walsh. J. O'Brien.
W. P. Quane. M. F. Ryan. W. P. Ryan. M. Harris. J. Heffernan. R. Butler.

CAHILL & CO., PRINTERS,   35, 36 & 37 GT. STRAND ST. DUBLIN.

The earliest known team photographs from Jones' Road. The woodland scene behind the players is a backdrop put up by the photographer but the fountain was a feature of Jones' Road.

encroach on the running of the GAA. Within its ranks a power struggle waged between the radical Irish Republican Brotherhood and the moderate constitutional nationalists for control of the Association. Even more damaging was the split in the Home Rule party caused by the party leader Charles Stewart Parnell's affair with Katharine O'Shea. While the GAA as a body lined up behind Parnell, the split in nationalist ranks was replicated in the ranks of the GAA, with deep divisions emerging at local level. Some clubs folded while others split along political lines. The disruption caused to the Association was nearly catastrophic. The GAA's annual convention for 1892 did not take place until 1893. The 1892 All-Ireland championships did not take place until 1893 and when they did, just three counties competed in the hurling and six in the football championship. According to Marcus de Búrca, in *The GAA: A History*, it is astonishing that the GAA survived at all.[3]

In addition to the political and administrative difficulties facing the GAA there were serious problems associated with the games themselves. The foundation of the GAA in 1884 was part of a European-wide movement for the establishment of games and sports on an organised basis. This trend was reflected in Ireland not just by the GAA but also by the founding of the Irish Rugby Football Union (1879), the Irish Football Association (1880) and the Irish Amateur Athletic Association (1885). These organised sports brought with them a demand by the public to watch the games. This was the era in which the modern phenomenon of spectator sports was born. For many years the demands of the public far outstripped the ability and resources of the organisers to accommodate them. This was true both in terms of playing facilities as well as in their ability even to accommodate all those who wanted to watch the matches. Indeed, the games were dogged by poor facilities, little or no crowd control and controversial decisions by officials. When the drama of sport was thrown into this volatile mix the scenes were at times comical, dangerous and chaotic as a survey of early All-Ireland finals reveals.

EARLY ALL-IRELANDS

The 1889 All-Ireland finals were played on 20 October 1889 on grounds owned by the Great Southern and Western Railway in Inchicore (today the site of Tyrconnell Park housing estate). Played on a waterlogged pitch in torrential rain, the football final was watched by over 3,000 spectators. It was a rough match and the crowd invaded the pitch time and time again resulting in many delays. Tipperary, represented again by Arravale Rovers, eventually won 3-6 to 0-0 – the only time a team has failed to score in a final. The hurling final was won by Dublin Kickhams. They defeated Tulla of Clare, who put themselves at a huge disadvantage by playing in bare feet.[4] The 1890 finals were not played until 26 June 1892 when both the hurling and football All-Irelands were contested at Clonturk Park in Drumcondra, Dublin. In the hurling final Midleton of Cork faced the Blues and Whites of Wexford. Just 1,000 people attended this All-Ireland, and all the players played barefoot. At half-time the Cork side led by 1-3 to 0-1. In the second half Wexford, apparently seeing no other hope for victory, resorted to injuring Cork players. Eight were injured in all. Eventually referee John Sheehy abandoned the match and awarded it to Cork. That night, bruised and battered, the Midleton team arrived back in Cork city by train. Cork's first All-Ireland champions arrived to a virtually empty platform. There were 'No musicians then, no teeming crowds to be held back by the police, no cheering, no excitement. Just a few questions from curious railway porters, anxious to shorten their night shift with a bit of conversation'.[5] The 1892 All-Irelands were played on 26 March 1893. In the football final Kerry's Laune Rangers met Dublin's Young Irelands. The Dublin crowd, while it was reported that they did not attempt violence, were extremely unsporting to their visitors leading to calls for no All-Irelands to be played in Dublin.[6] The hurling final was also played on the same day. Availing of a new ruling allowing the county champions to select players from other teams – this was the start of proper county teams – the Redmonds of Cork selected players from Blackrock and Aghabullogue to line out against the Dublin Faughs. At half-time Cork led 4 points to no score. After the restart Cork scored a disputed goal. The Faughs argued that the ball had already crossed the point line before crossing the goal line (see below). Amidst chaotic scenes the referee Dan Fraher, unsure of how to proceed, announced he would defer the decision about the score to a later meeting of the Central Council of the GAA. However, by the time he had announced this compromise many of the Dublin players had left thus making a restart impossible. Cork were awarded the title.[7] The 1893 All-Irelands were scheduled to take place on 24 June 1894 at the Ashtown Trotting Grounds northwest of the Phoenix

Park. On the day over 1,000 people had paid into the grounds only to find it totally unsuitable for hurling – there were no pitch markings and the grass was knee high. Faced with such conditions the teams refused to play. Undeterred, some of the stronger players uprooted the goalposts and made their way to the Phoenix Park where the games were successfully concluded. The football match was regarded as one of the hardest and dourest finals of all time. It ended controversially when, in the second half, the Young Irelands of Wexford alleged that a Cork player had deliberately downed one of their team and kicked him on the head while he lay on the ground. The crowd, as usual unimpeded by any sort of fencing, invaded the pitch. The referee ordered the replacement of both players but Cork walked off in protest and Wexford were awarded the match.[8] The 1894 football final was played between Dublin and Cork at Clonturk Park in Drumcondra. With the scores level at full-time the referee ordered extra time to be played. Cork refused to play on. Subsequently Central Council ordered a replay at the neutral venue of Thurles on 21 April. Over 10,000 people were present at the replay including Archbishop Croke, the principal patron of the association. Notwithstanding the presence of such a figure, the crowd invaded the pitch with Cork leading 1-2 to 0-5 (at the time a goal exceeded any number of points). Dublin refused to continue. When Central Council ordered another replay Cork refused to play and Dublin were declared champions.[9]

Events surrounding the 1895 football final were even more bizarre. Played on 21 March 1896 this was the first final to be held at the Jones' Road venue. A huge crowd attended but there were no pitch invasions, fights or disputes during the game. As a result the game lasted just sixty-eight minutes including the interval – a remarkably short period of time when interrupted matches often could last more than two hours. Among the crowd that day was the Welsh international rugby team, in Dublin for a match, who 'expressed themselves highly pleased with the decorum of the players, which was so much at variance with the reports they have from time to time heard of our pastimes'. On the day Arravale Rovers of Tipperary beat the Leinster champions Meath, represented by Navan O'Mahonys, four points to three. However, in a remarkable turn of events the referee, J.J. Kenny, wrote a letter to the *Irish Independent* the day after the match stating that Tipperary's second point was illegal. He explained that the player who scored the point was not outside the 21-yard mark when Meath kicked out from goal. From his illegal position this player intercepted the ball and scored a point. Kenny asserted in the letter that the game should have ended in a draw (he wrote the letter because 'I had to have my say out or I would have burst').[10] Addressing the matter a week later Central Council decided that the result should stand but a special set of medals would be given to the Meath team as Leinster champions.[11]

INCREASED POPULARITY OF THE GAMES

In the second half of the 1890s the fortunes of the GAA began to improve. By the turn of the century there was a new vigour evident in the association. Although politics will always form part of the context to such an organisation as the GAA, the near catastrophic divisions of the 1890s had begun to heal by the turn of the century. At the same time the centenary celebrations of the 1798 Rebellion and the continued rise of cultural nationalism, especially in the form of the Gaelic League, provided a healthy backdrop to the expansion of the GAA. Added to this was the emergence of a new generation of leadership in the GAA. In September 1901 the GAA's Annual Congress elected Jim Nowlan of Kilkenny President and Luke O'Toole was made Secretary. Nowlan held office for

Jim Nowlan (left) was appointed President of the GAA and Luke O'Toole was appointed Secretary, September 1901.

twenty years and O'Toole served as Secretary for twenty-eight years (1901–1929). Nowlan and O'Toole found the association at its lowest point but the two revived it and guided it through its first great period of expansion. In addition the games benefited from a champion with a pen in his hand, P.J. Devlin, who, writing under the pseudonym 'Celt', was a strong advocate of Gaelic games in the press. On the field Michael Crowe of Limerick tried to address the serious problem of lack of uniformity in the interpretation of the rules of the games – a problem which still causes controversy although the variations today are slight by comparison.[12] For over two decades he travelled tirelessly as a referee 'to make the games more scientific as public spectacles'. In a comment on his success at the job he replied, 'I know human nature very well'.[13] An important development in administration was the establishment of the four provincial councils between 1900 and 1903.

These changes were welcome improvements but the success of Gaelic games did not rely solely on political and administrative considerations. The actual playing of the games was, of course, crucial and in this area there were many positive developments. The way the games were played changed considerably in the early years. Originally each team consisted of twenty-one players, thus making the field congested. The scoring system was similar, consisting of goals and points, but there were a couple of differences. The goal area stood between two side posts similar to today's international rules. Any score between the posts and outside the goal area was a point. However, in the early days a goal wiped out any number of points so points only mattered when the teams were level on goals. Since there were no nets in the goal it was difficult to know whether a goal or point had been scored and confusion was compounded by the lack of flags to signal the type of score. In the days before the solo run football players were allowed to run only four paces with the ball or to hop the ball once to clear it after catching. Wrestling and tripping were allowed and headlong rushes were a feature. Indeed, there was more than a passing resemblance to American football or rugby with lots of fumbling and scrambling. There were very few frees in the games, thus resulting in some very low-scoring games. In 1931 'Celt' commented that 'the whistle seldom sounded in those days, when it took fitness and courage to enter the championship arena'.[14] During the first couple of decades of the new century the rules of the games changed on a number of occasions. The number on a team was reduced first to seventeen and then finally to fifteen which improved the speed of the games. Hurling benefited greatly from lighter sliotars. Nets were introduced in goals. The side posts were dispensed with and the familiar posts of today were introduced. A goal was made equal to at first five points and then finally three.

Partly as a result of the changes in the association and the developments in the rules the games became increasingly popular both in terms of the numbers playing and the numbers watching. By 1909 every county in Ireland had a board affiliated to the Central Council. The games were now becoming embedded in the social fabric of the nation. Reflecting their popularity the attendances at Gaelic games were the largest of any sporting fixture in Ireland. One rugby supporter, used to the smaller attendance at Lansdowne Road, went to sample a day at Jones' Road. He recounted, 'I managed to make struggle and be fully attired by eleven o'clock, at which hour I commenced to wend my way to the scene of this all-important fixture, where to my great surprise, I saw multitudes flocking for admission, and it was quite twenty minutes before my turn came to reach the turnstiles at the entrance to Jones' Road.'[15]

Ultimately the essential ingredient for success was of course great games on the fields of play. It was in this increasingly favourable environment that some crucial matches were played in both hurling and football. Two of the most important hurling matches to be played during these years were All-Ireland finals involving London-Irish teams. In 1901 England was made a GAA 'province' and a short-lived new championship structure was established in which there was a 'Home Final', the winner of which would play the exile selection for the All-Ireland title. The 1901 final was played at Jones' Road on 26 October 1902 in front of 8,000 spectators. The 'exiles' travelled from England with the assistance of a Central Council grant of £70 (to help keep costs down preference was given during selection to players who could play in both the football and hurling matches). The teams' boat arrived in Dublin at 2 am on the morning of the match and docked at the North Wall. The men, 'weary, travel-stained, but jolly' were put up in the North Star hotel. Despite a less arduous journey the Tipperary team arrived in Dublin at 1 pm – the scheduled start-time – and it was not until 2.10 that the Lord Mayor of Dublin, Tim Harrington, MP, threw in the ball. Despite fears that all that could be hoped for was a fair contest between the men of Tipperary and a disparate group who

Páidí Ó Sé

FORMER KERRY FOOTBALLER (WINNER OF EIGHT ALL-IRELANDS),
FORMER KERRY, WESTMEATH AND CLARE MANAGER

I remember leaving Kerry with Pat Spillane on our way to see the All-Ireland Final of 1972 when Kerry played Offaly. We were boarders in St Brendan's College in Killarney at the time. We didn't return on the Sunday night and got accommodation close to Croke Park before we hit off down town. We were walking by Croke Park later, heading for the house where we were staying, when to our surprise we noticed the gate to the field open. We ran in and onto the pitch for our first run ever on the famous sod. It felt great running up and down but we had no ball to kick. Before long though we imagined we had an O'Neills ball. Pat went into the left-corner forward position and I kicked a great ball into him. He fielded the imaginary ball well, turned on the spot and shot over the bar. I fielded the kick-out in the moonlight and this time placed the kick wide of Pat on the outside. I kept yelling at him as he went like hell after the ball and scored again. It was mighty fun until we stopped and headed for the bed, wondering would we be expelled from Brendan's when we got home some time on Monday.

The strange thing is we were both back playing for Kerry in an All-Ireland final three years later when we won our first senior All-Ireland medal by beating Dublin. Pat played in that same corner as he did that night and scored four points. The practice obviously stood to him.

played on foreign fields, the largest crowd yet seen at Jones' Road assembled. As one spectator recounted there were mixed feelings in the crowd:

> Two conflicting emotions swayed many of the vast assemblage at Jones's Road … in a desire to see the merits and the dash of the 'exiles' rewarded by victory; and an apprehension of the hurling championship being carried to England. It was strange, and at the same time discordant, to

hear vociferous shouts of 'Go on London' from a Gaelic crowd to as magnificent a team of hurlers as ever graced a Gaelic green or enthralled a hurling-loving populace. A hundred distracting thoughts rushed through one's brain during the scene ...

Contrary to expectations the game was the best, closest and fastest hurling final yet to have been played. At half-time Tipperary led the London-Irish five points to three. Cheered on by many of the neutrals in the crowd, the exiles fought back in the second half. When they took the lead 'pandemonium reigned' and the barriers holding back the crowd gave way, although the field was quickly cleared. However, in the last minutes Tipperary scored a goal to seal victory. At the final whistle 'there was a wild rush of spectators; victor and vanquished were stormed by admirers'.[16]

In the following year London-Irish returned to play Redmonds of Cork on 2 August 1903. Ironically the London team was made up almost totally of Munster men with the majority of the team hailing from Cork; the fraternity between the teams was shown when they walked out onto the pitch at Jones' Road arm in arm. The match was played in dreadful conditions with 'a sodden ground, incessant rain, and a greasy ball'. Each of the skills required to play hurling was made difficult. The teams were level at half-time but remarkably London won the match 1-5 to 0-4. The All-Ireland title went abroad for the first and last time. According to one writer, 'some of the Cork team seemed absolutely bewildered, and not infrequently failed to hit the ball when quite alone, and, towards the end of the second period they tired palpably, whether from the heavy going or disgust, we cannot tell'.[17]

While hurling benefited greatly from these finals, a turning point in the history of football came in 1905 when the 1903 All-Ireland final was contested over three games by Kildare and Kerry. This was the first All-Ireland that really succeeded in capturing the popular imagination and it was these encounters that were almost immediately recognised as making Gaelic football a modern spectator sport. Kerry, made up largely from Killarney and Tralee players, and Kildare, made up from players from Clane and Roseberry, had built up contrasting styles of play that favoured an expansive game rather than what had been the norm of headlong rushes with the ball at the players' feet. According to one writer, 'The kingdom brought thoughtful, accurate kicking alternately to wing and centre with

Kerry (Tralee) Football Team. Winners of 1903 Munster Championship.

.F. O'Sullivan. E. O'Sullivan. R. Kirwan.   J. Myers.   D. Kissane.   A. Stack.   C. Healy.   M. M'Carthy.   T. Looney.   J. P. O'S
on.Sec.Co.Bd.   Pres.Co.Bd.   Hon. Sec.
        D. Curran.   C. Duggan.   D. M'Carthy.   T. O'Gorman.   J. Buckley.   W. Lynch.   P. Dillon.
                                              Captain.
        J. O'Gorman   R. Fitzgerald   J. T. Fitzgerald   D. Breen.

Kerry (Tralee), winners of the 1903 Munster Championship, who won the 1903 All-Ireland final after two replays.

brainy shooting within range [while] Kildare … introduced well-conceived passing by hand and foot in attack with weaving movements in unison around goal'.[18] Unusually each team undertook special training for the match.

The first game was played in Tipperary town on 23 July. A crowd of between 12–15,000 was estimated to have watched the match. Although a watershed in the development of the game, there were some of the familiar problems – no stands or embankments and just a rope holding the spectators back from the pitch. At half-time Kerry were leading by two points to one. The restart was delayed until the crowd was cleared from the pitch. In the second half Kildare scored a controversial goal when a line of Kildare supporters encroached on the pitch and the Kildare wings went behind them. The Kerry team thought the ball had gone dead and were caught unawares when the Kildare players re-emerged from behind the supporters and scored a goal. Kerry then scored a disputed goal. The Kerry fans invaded the pitch in jubilation. When he was unable to clear the pitch the referee declared Kerry the winners 1-4 to 1-3. Subsequently

Co. Kildare Team G.A.A., Clane. Winners of Leinster Championship, 1903.

W. J. RANKIN.   J. MURRAY.   L. CRIBBON   J. GORMAN.   M'MURRAY.   J. WRIGHT.   R. J. RADLEY.
Hon. Sec. Co. Committee.
F. COSLAN.   J. SCOTT.   M. DONNELLY.   J. FITZGERALD.   M. FITZGERALD.   J. P. LACEY, Hon. Sec.
E. KENNEDY.   M. KENNEDY.   J. RAFFERTY.   W. BRACKEN.   W. LOSTY.   W. MERRIMAN.

Copyright

Kildare (Clane), winners of the 1903 Leinster Championship, who lost to Kerry in the 1903 All-Ireland. The three games played to decide the winner were regarded as a turning point in the popularity of Gaelic football.

Central Council ordered a replay with Cork as the venue. In the replay Kildare scored a last-minute goal to level the scores 1-4 to 0-7.

The second replay was again set for Cork. By this time the country was enthralled. Media interest in the replay was unprecedented. One example of this was the *Leinster Leader* that had devoted a mere twenty-one lines to the first match. By the second replay much of the newspaper was given over to the match. Cork city was thronged with supporters of the two counties and 25,000 people produced a gate of £270. According to the *Kerry Sentinal,* 'it was a great struggle in every respect and has done more to awaken an intelligent interest in our national past-times and to increase the respect of the Shoneens and other undesirables for our games than any

Scenes from the second replay of the epic 1903 football final between Kerry and Kildare.

dozen of the most important fixtures ever held under the auspices of the Association'[19]. While the game marked the emergence of Kerry as a force in Gaelic football, more significantly it signalled a bright new era for Gaelic football.

THE NEED FOR BETTER FACILITIES

Against the background of advances in many aspects of the games the issue of poor grounds continued to plague the association and to hamper the growth of the games. In July 1904 the All-Ireland football final was held in Kilkenny. According to one journalist the ground was 'not at all suited for such an important match', with no proper enclosures which resulted in frequent incursions by the crowd onto the pitch.[20] In Limerick there was a particular problem with people sneaking into the grounds without paying. Known as 'wall-climbers and gate-breakers', they were more interested in causing disruption than watching the match.[21] The 1903 Leinster hurling semi-final between Wexford and Kilkenny was a near disaster with the crowds breaking down the entrance to the ground allowing a large number to get in free. During the game a fight between two players led to a general mêlée as the crowd became involved. It was lamented that:

> … some effort would not be made to make Jones' Road an enclosed ground in the true sense of the word. As it is, there is unfortunately very little trouble in getting in without paying; and that is not the worst of it, for the wall-climbers are sometimes very careless about their conduct when inside, especially when in any large numbers. They make common cause to defy all authority, go where they wish, and stand where they like.[22]

The inadequacies of Jones' Road were again highlighted at a challenge match between Dublin and Tipperary in February 1905 when a huge crowd of over 15,000 attended. The grounds, stands and enclosures were described as a 'mass of humanity'. As the stands and enclosures only went half way round the pitch the majority of the people had to go into the non-railed area. The referee stopped the match on two occasions due to pitch invasions. However, in one report on the match it was written that the crowd could not 'be reasonably blamed for any little encroachment of the grounds … when people are lined from six to eight deep on a side-line without a barrier in front, and all anxious – most keenly so – to witness the play, it is impossible for stewards to keep back the crowd'.[23] At a match at Jones' Road between Kerry and Dublin in 1906 the habit of

Tony O'Hehir

COMMENTATOR AND JOURNALIST, SON OF COMMENTATOR
MICHEÁL O'HEHIR

For years Tommy Reilly, a friend of my father, kept the scores for my father wherever he went 'commentating'. When Tommy got old I was brought along to do the same job and it was always very exciting. A man called Jack Keating was one of the RTÉ technicians of the time and Dad was always a little bit nervous if Jack happened to be on duty when Dublin were playing. He had reason to be so because Jack was a committed Dublin fan. He reacted as genuine followers do and on one occasion when Dublin were playing the great Down team of the 1960s he jumped up in the box in protest at a blatant foul on a Dublin player. But in so doing all the wires attached to mikes and headphones were stretched beyond limits and nearly strangled the commentator there and then.

I remember being with him the day that referee Eamonn Moules made the famous decision giving a free out to Galway rather than the intended penalty to Neilly Gallagher of Donegal.

Like everybody in the ground my father was wondering why the ref had changed his mind.

He often thought it funny to have 'loads of room' in the box for the early rounds of the championship and would remark when coming in on bigger days that 'we will be well looked after today'. It was a serious job to be keeping the scores for him and there was no 'place' for a display of excitement. It happened to me once when Dublin were playing and while he could not say anything at the time, the fierce look I got told me clearly that I had 'fouled'.

He had great regard for the Down team of the 1960s. I would say that Sean Purcell of Galway was his favourite player, but he was not biased. But on one occasion I do remember three Dublin fans calling to our house in Griffith Avenue before the 1963 final between Dublin and Galway and stating that it was wrong for him to have a maroon coloured car.

He never liked the new fashion of hurlers wearing helmets. Helmets took away some of the personality of the players – was there a point any longer in referring to a hurler as being dark or fair-haired when it was all covered up?

'wall-climbers' making the ground a 'common' was stifled by a number of hurlers brought in for security duty.[24]

It was apparent that something needed to be done about where the games were played. One of the priorities was a suitable venue for the All-Ireland finals. The finals had been something of a roadshow, with a host of venues used in twenty years. Venues in Dublin apart from Jones' Road included the ground owned by Lord Ffrench at Elm Park, Beech Hill, Clonskeagh (the venue for the first football All-Ireland), Inchicore, the Phoenix Park, the natural amphitheatre of Clonturk Park situated on the north side of the city not too far from the City and Suburban Sports grounds (this had been a favourite location for many) and the Gaelic Park on the Kimmage Road, Terenure, which was described as 'well and carefully laid out and situated in a beautiful locality, hedged with trees, with a beautiful fresh green sward, the whole surroundings are very pretty'. Locations outside Dublin included Birr, a field in Carrick-on-Suir owned by Maurice Davin, a founder of the GAA, St James' Park in Kilkenny, the grounds of the Agricultural Society in Athy and Pat McGrath's field in Tipperary town. In Dublin the closing of the Nine Acres in the Phoenix Park and the Terenure venue to Gaelic games led the newspaper *Sport* to state that it was 'surely time that the Gael's were independent' and not susceptible to the whims of others in deciding where they could play their games.[25] Calls came for the association to gain control over playing fields. The need for a major venue was paramount but it was by no means certain where this would be. Dublin may seem the obvious choice in retrospect but things were not so clear-cut at the time. Of the twenty-two hurling finals (and replays) played between 1887 and 1907, twelve were held outside Dublin. Of the twenty-three football finals (and replays) twelve were held outside Dublin. Of the finals played outside Dublin all but four were played in Munster. In fact the trend had been increasingly away from Dublin for the finals. Between 1900 and 1908 only two finals had been played in Dublin – they were both played in Terenure. However, despite the Munster roots of the Association it was perhaps inevitable that due to demographics and transport Dublin would be chosen. In 1904 and 1909 respectively there were significant straws in the wind when Central Council set up its offices at 68 Upper O'Connell Street in Dublin and Annual Congress was transferred to Dublin.[26]

SURGEON McARDLE, STAR
——— AT JONES' ROAD,

FRANK DINEEN BUYS JONES' ROAD

In April 1907 an ideal opportunity arose when the ground at Jones' Road was put up for auction. The venue had been on the decline for a few years and the owners had been anxious to find a lucrative alternative use for the land. In November 1904 Dublin Corporation turned down the opportunity to buy the land to build artisan cottages. After the owner of the land, Alderman Maurice Butterly, died the property was put up for sale in 1907. However, the GAA, given their tight financial position, did not make an offer for what was obviously an attractive venue. On the day

THE IRISH MARATHON,
AY 16TH 1909.

Surgeon McArdle starting the Irish marathon at Jones' Road, 16 May 1909. The man on the far right is believed to be Frank Dineen, the then owner of Croke Park.

there was no suitable bid so the sale was postponed and private negotiations were entered into with Frank Dineen. Dineen bought the grounds at Jones' Road for £3,250.

At the time of the Jones' Road sale Dineen was President of the GAA's Athletics Council – he was the first to hold the post. Born in Ballylanders, County Limerick, and educated at Rockwell College, he worked as a journalist for the *Freeman's Journal*, *Sport* and the *Evening Telegraph*. A renowned athlete in the 1880s he excelled in sprinting – he once held the national record for the 100 yards – and the high jump. When rival athletic bodies were set up Dineen was put under strong pressure by members of

Frank Dineen.

the Irish Amateur Athletic Association not to join the GAA. However, he competed in the GAA's first big athletics meeting at Blarney, Cork (he won the 100 yards in a time of 10 3/5 seconds as well as the high jump). After retiring from competition he became a handicapper and handicapped all the principal meetings of Irish athletics. He also became a prominent member of Central Council of the GAA and was elected President in 1895 and then Secretary of the Association in 1898 – Dineen is the only person to have held these two most important offices. Although a GAA man and acting out of his own beliefs that the Association needed its own ground buying the grounds was very much his own initiative. In his newspaper articles he had long lamented the inadequacy of the GAA's venues. From today's perspective buying the grounds was an inspired move by someone who saw that a mass spectator sport needed proper facilities for both the spectators and the players.

Having purchased Jones' Road Dineen set out to improve its facilities, putting his own ideas into practice. He was to spend considerably and, although he received £10 rent for each major event, Dineen was forced by his precarious financial position to sell four acres of the land at Jones' Road to the Jesuits of Belvedere College for £1,090 in 1910. There were many compliments made about the changes. An article reporting on the Irish Professional Athletics championships held in Jones' Road commented that 'the popular venue never looked in better trim, and despite the heavy soaking which the track [had] received, it was in capital order'.[27] In the 1 May 1909 edition of *Sport* it was reported that the 6–7,000 spectators who attended the All-Ireland hurling final at Jones' Road on the previous day 'must have rubbed their eyes in astonishment and asked themselves were they in the right place. The new proprietor has spared neither expense nor architectural skill in laying out the grounds, and as an athletic arena it is now second to none in the Three Kingdoms, and the many thousands that assembled must have felt sincerely proud of the headquarters of Gaelic

An athletics race at Jones' Road in the 1910s, with the pavilion stand in the background. The railway wall can be seen in the distance.

sport in Ireland. The grounds have been so arranged that no matter how large the attendance, every individual can see the play with comfort, and as for the players, the playing pitch has been levelled and rolled, so that first-class hurling is made a certainty of.'[28] The game ended in a draw, Tipperary 2-5 Dublin 1-8, and although Jones' Road was such a success its supremacy as the main venue for the association was not yet established and the replay was set for Athy.

In December 1909, the football final between Louth and Kerry attracted great interest. In anticipation of the game special arrangements were made; reserved sideline seats could be purchased in advance for 2s 6d each from Central Council offices at O'Connell Street, sixty stewards were appointed for the day and were requested to be in attendance ninety minutes before the throw in, special ticket arrangements were made to minimise crushing and confusion at the turnstiles and special arrangements were made for the parking of hackneys and private motor cars. The largest crowd yet to witness a match at the venue attended – 'a view from the field of play showed people everywhere, on tops of houses, on tops of walls, up

Martin White

FORMER KILKENNY HURLER WHO PLAYED IN FIVE ALL-IRELANDS BETWEEN
1931 AND 1937, WINNING THREE OF THEM

My first match in Croke Park was the Leinster Colleges final of 1925 between St Kiernan's College and Blackrock College. We won and I remember our trainer Fr Billy Dunne taking off his collar and hanging it on his walking stick which he stuck in the ground while running up and down the sideline. The Blackrock crowd had a great following and kept shouting 'Rock! Rock! Rock!', all the time. We beat Newbridge College in the final the following year and that was in Croke Park too.

It was a far different place to what it is today. There was a small stand in the corner and the first Hogan but the rest of the place was a green bank – the Hill, all down the Cusack side, in front of the Canal and a bit of the Hogan side.

The dressing rooms were ordinary rooms under the small Hogan Stand and there was not even a wash basin or electric light. But I remember the pitch was excellent because Chicky Curran was very proud of it. He never liked to be called Chicky but everyone did and his son Jimmy was as good as him when he became groundsman later.

The place had not changed much when I played in the All-Ireland final of 1931 against Cork, which they won. But we won the finals of 1932, 1933 and 1935. 1935 was the best of all because Lory Meagher was captain and everyone wanted to see him as a winning captain towards the end of a career. I was lucky and scored the winning goal. Lory had a great style of his own with a long easy swing like a good golfer. He looked slow but he was always where the ball was and seemed to have plenty of time to strike it. It was a very wet day and before the match started our full-back, Peter Reilly, even came to me to see would I ask Lory to call it off. I remember taking my boots off at half-time and turning them upside down to let the water out.

We used to stay in the Ossory Hotel on the night before the finals and a big crowd would gather outside on the Sunday morning cheering. They would wait and walk with us to Croke Park – a huge crowd. It was great for the nerves and tension – you would know most of them and they would be shouting and encouraging you. It helped too that our local bands like the Kells Pipers and the Saint Patrick's Brass and Reed Band played on the day as well as the Artane Band.

We only came together to train a few times during the fortnight before a final and an odd time for a semi-final. A couple of rounds of the field, a few sprints and a bit of hurling was all that was involved.

We had great times in Croke Park and made good friends like the Mackeys – Mick and John – and Jackie Power from Limerick and Vestie Muldowney from Dublin. Vestie was the first man I saw somersaulting after a score like the soccer players do now.

telegraph and telephone posts – the whole place seemed a living mass of humanity, but the order was perfect, and the field of play as free from encroachment as if there were none but the players present'. It was 'a great day for everyone' and a 'magnificent triumph of the Association'.[29] Dineen had made Jones' Road the main venue for the Association. In the seven years after he purchased it all but one of the hurling and football finals were played there.

CROKE MEMORIAL CUP FINAL

In 1913 a Croke Memorial Tournament was organised to raise funds for a suitable monument to the first patron of the association, Archbishop Croke, who had died in 1902. On 16 February 1913 matches took place at several venues throughout the country. The numbers of counties taking part in the Tournament were small, just nine in football and five in hurling, but these counties were considered the best in the country.[30] Such was their calibre that the Croke Memorial Tournament was put on a par with that year's All-Ireland

Founding patron of the GAA, Archbishop Croke, after whom the Jones' Road venue was renamed in 1913.

championships. Interest in the football was particularly high as it seemed to be written in the competition's script that the final would be a long-awaited re-match between the rivals of Louth and Kerry. Louth and Kerry had fought out the 1909 All-Ireland at Jones' Road with Kerry winning on that occasion. The 'wee county' and 'the kingdom' were set for a replay in the 1910 final. However, Kerry were in dispute with the Great Southern and Western Railway and refused to travel so Louth were declared champions. Their re-match, scheduled for 4 May 1913, aroused huge interest. According to one newspaper article, 'there was never a match more welcomed by both sides and by the neutral public'.[31]

In anticipation of the largest crowd yet at Jones' Road Dineen busied himself making modifications. Behind the Clonliffe Road goal rails were

MY MEMORIES

Eamon Moules

FORMER ALL-IRELAND REFEREE

I refereed several Leinster finals and at the All-Ireland finals of 1962 and 1963 but the one game that I will never forget is the League semi-final of 1967 between Galway and Donegal. The wind was fairly strong when I blew for a Donegal penalty into the Railway Goal but the wind was not a factor in what happened afterwards.

The ball was placed in the correct spot but nobody moved to take the kick. The wind then blew the ball towards the goal and I told 'him' to replace it and this was done. There was still hesitation and I blew the whistle for the kick to be taken. Then Neilly Gallagher walked up – picked up the ball and replaced it once more.

I immediately blew and signalled for a free out for handling the ball on the ground as per the rule of the time. It was harsh but as far as I was concerned 'rules is rules'. It would be a 'hop ball' according to the current rules.

That penalty incident was not the only thing from that match brought to my notice subsequently. I met Johnny Geraghty, the Galway goal-keeper, in New York later on when I was refereeing the League final and he mentioned that one of my Croke Park umpires 'that day' would not talk to him about how much time was left or anything else either. The umpire in question was Denis Doyle. He was the best at the job of umpire I ever had but he was both deaf and dumb. When I informed Johnny in New York he felt sort of embarrassed.

put up to keep the crowd off the playing area while a large part of the area around the pitch was banked and extended. It was estimated that the changes increased capacity by 10,000. Such was the expected demand for accommodation that Central Council withdrew the usual policy of allowing ladies free admission. Admission to the Canal End was six pence, and 1,000 sideline seats were one shilling and six pence.[32] On the day 'The crowded state of the streets of the city was a result of the incursions of our country cousins and had the effect of drawing to the match many who would not otherwise think – or, more accurately, might be forgetful of the importance of the occasion … Outside the gates the scene was very interesting. All sorts of conveyances lined the roads leading to the grounds, and one would have thought that the drivers of almost all the hackney cars in the city had concentrated on Jones' Road. Motors and taxi-cabs were also in strong array'.[33] The game could not have been tighter. Scores were level at half-time and again at the final whistle.

The replay was scheduled for 29 June at Jones' Road. In preparation each team used a special trainer. The Kerry team were based in Tralee and did one hour of sprints each morning, a walk to Fenit around midday and then evening practice on the sports field.[34] Large numbers of Louth supporters gathered to watch their team train each day.[35] Meanwhile, at Jones' Road, further changes were being made. Among the preparations was the increase of the banking to contain several thousand more supporters and the erection of two new stands in the enclosure to seat a further 3,000, while Central Council erected their own stands for the day. Harry Boland, Luke O'Toole and Michael Crowe (three leading figures of the GAA) cast their eye over arrangements and declared themselves very pleased.[36]

While people from Kerry and Louth, of course, accounted for the bulk of supporters in attendance special trains from all parts of the country brought interested neutrals to Dublin. Kingsbridge (now Heuston station) and Amiens Street (now Connolly station) were teeming with over 21,000 supporters who had travelled by train. Kingsbridge had a predominance of gold and green while at Amiens Street 'almost everybody, young and old, sported the colours of Louth in buttons, badges and various devices'.[37] At Jones' Road 200 stewards were on duty and when the gates were opened at 1.40 for the 3.00 start thousands were already waiting. The replay was attended by a record 32,000 spectators – with many more watching free from the Great Southern and Western Railway line;

Never before did the familiar tryst at Jones' Road, with its long association with the foremost fixtures, present such a spectacle of massed, expectant, enthusiastic, palpitating humanity … The scene was one to be witnessed, and being witnessed to remain indelibly fixed in the memory … Everything else paled into paltriness compared with the match. Jones' Road was the one objective in the city. Nothing was talked of but the chances of the contest.

With a politician's appreciation of an opportunity to press the flesh, John Redmond, leader of the Irish Parliamentary Party, was in the crowd. On his arrival he received a standing ovation and was given the honour of being introduced to the team captains. However, the replay did not live up to the expectations generated by the first. With the teams level at half-time Kerry went on to win by 2-4 to 0-5.[38]

GAA PURCHASES JONES' ROAD

The windfall from the Croke Memorial Tournament presented the GAA with a unique opportunity. The gate receipts from the record attendance gave a huge boost to the memorial fund. It rose from £500 to nearly £2,400. It had been assumed, especially by those in Tipperary, that the funds would go towards a suitable memorial in Thurles. However, Central Council quickly made it clear that the monies would be used to purchase a ground to be called after the late patron. After much discussion at Central

The 1913 All-Ireland pre-match parade involving Kerry and Wexford.

Council and in negotiations with the Tipperary County Board it was decided that £300 would be spent on a new hall in Thurles – to be called Croke Memorial Hall – with £2,400 to be used for the purchase of a ground in Dublin to be called the 'Croke Memorial Park Ground'. However, it was by no means sure that they would purchase Jones' Road. In *The GAA: A History* it is suggested that Dineen's relationship with the GAA was a difficult one. In August 1913 a three-man committee was set up to judge the respective merits of Jones' Road (with a price of £4,000) and the larger property at Elm Park (for £5,000). For a time it seemed as if the south-side venue would be chosen – how that might have changed the fortunes of Gaelic games in the capital! Dineen, fearing a lost sale, dropped his asking price first to £3,625 and then finally to £3,500. In an 8-7 vote at Central Council on 4 October it was decided to purchase Jones' Road.[39]

One month after the decision was made to purchase Jones' Road the GAA advertised that the 1913 All-Irelands would be played in 'Croke Memorial Ground'. However, it was not until after the football final that the GAA actually took ownership of the ground. In the hurling final

Mooncoin of Kilkenny defeated Toomyvara of Tipperary and Kerry beat Wexford in the football final. The crowds at the finals were lower than normal because it was during the Lockout and there was no labour available to erect temporary stands.[40]

On 22 December 1913 ownership of the ground passed over to the GAA. Including legal fees, the total cost of the purchase was £3,641. The GAA finally had a home of its own.

CHAPTER TWO
1914–1924

Preparing to enter Croke Park at the opening of the 1924 Tailteann Games.

Croke Park is as much about memory as it is about live action. The memories of heroes, of victories and of defeats infuse the arena with a cocktail of emotions beyond the drama, and ebb and flow, of the match being played. Probably the most potent of the sporting emotions are those distilled by lack of success. There are none more powerful than the deep yearnings embedded by years of humiliating defeats and might-have-beens. How people wait for the day when the philosophical summations after loss can be cast aside and victory thoughtlessly embraced.

Few counties' experiences illustrate the impact of memory and absence more than Clare. On 18 October 1914 they played in the first All-Ireland hurling final held in the GAA-owned Croke Park. Appropriately they came up against Laois, also an All-Ireland debutant. Clare ran out winners 5-1 to 1-0. The victory was deceptively easy. The next time Clare were crowned All-Ireland champions was eighty-one years later when they beat Offaly at Croke Park. The memory of 1914 figured strongly in the build up. Many of the 1995 Clare team and their supporters had heard of men like Pat 'Fowler' McInerney, Jack Shadoo, Ned Grace and Martin Maloney who

The Clare team who won the 1914 All-Ireland hurling final. It was the first All-Ireland held in the GAA-owned Croke Park.

were led out by Willie Redmond MP in Croke Park in the early days of the First World War. In 1995 Tom Humphries wrote in *The Irish Times,* 'Seldom can an All-Ireland have been so yearned for, so passionately willed and wanted. At the end, the faithful poured onto the pitch and created a din to raise the dead generations of Clare people who thought this day would never come'. When team captain Anthony Daly accepted the cup he made the traditional speech on the steps of the Hogan Stand. Certainly he felt the hand of sporting history on his shoulder when he said there were better Clare teams who had preceded them and he was accepting the cup on their behalf. When he said that Liam MacCarthy had been missing from Clare for eighty-one years the sentiment was correct. However, the MacCarthy trophy was only presented for the first time in 1923.[1]

In contrast to the novel pairing of the 1914 hurling final the first football final at Croke Memorial Park was between Kerry and Wexford, two counties who were to become very familiar with Croke Park (albeit in different codes). Their struggle on 1 November 1914 was an epic encounter played before 13,000 spectators. Harry Boland, who was later to feature prominently in the War of Independence, refereed the match. The last fifteen minutes saw a colossal struggle for supremacy with 'Greek meeting Greek', as one report put it.[2] Kerry salvaged a draw with a last-minute free. The replay attracted 21,000 to Croke Park. The crowd began arriving at noon and by two o'clock 'every available point of vantage was secured'.[3] A gale-force wind dominated proceedings with all the scores going with the wind. At half-time Wexford led 0-6 to 0-0, but Kerry ran up 2-3 without reply in the second half.

In a meeting of Central Council in June 1914 the issue of Croke Park was raised. One point that had to be resolved was the legal effects of the purchase. The GAA as an organisation had no legal basis. This meant that the ground belonged to the individuals who had negotiated the deal. They were, of course, also personally liable for any debts. To regularise this situation the GAA became a limited company on 7 September 1914.

Now that the GAA had its own grounds for showcase events, Central Council lost little time in effecting improvements to what was and remains the Association's most valuable asset. The grounds bought by the GAA had only the most basic facilities. The pitch was uneven, the only fixed seating areas were a small uncovered stand and a pavilion (then called the 'grand stand') on the Jones' Road side with other vantage points being on mounds of earth. Among the immediate changes was the demolition of half the old timber stand. This was replaced by a large earthen embankment which it was intended to cover once it had been made firm by 'the traffic of spectators and the weather'. Right round the rest of the ground the banking had been increased, especially at the Great Southern and Western Railway end.[4] The installation of 1,500 new sideline seats at a cost of £115 immediately paid for themselves – the sale of these seats for the 1914 football final took in £300. Other alterations included the construction of concrete walls at Jones' Road (400 feet long and 17 1/2 feet high) and at the Clonliffe end. Both were built to stop people getting in free.[5]

In 1919 a Croke Park management committee was appointed to oversee a second phase of works as well as other matters relating to the stadium.[6] After some months they agreed a works scheme and asked Secretary Luke O'Toole to interview architects to carry it out. To help cover costs a 'monster tournament' was organised. Among the changes was the re-sodding of the pitch, the construction of a railing the full circumference of the pitch and a new stand. Matches for the 'Croke Park Tournament' took place at a number of locations in March 1920. However, due to political circumstances it was not completed until December 1921. By this time, the GAA had run into significant debts arising from its improvements at Croke Park. In recognition of the role that the organisation played in the national movement the Dáil cabinet approved a financial package for the GAA. Their debt of £1,700 was to be paid off and they were given a loan of £6,000 at a low interest rate.[7] The major asset of the GAA had been saved.

Shortly after the GAA purchased Croke Park the First World War broke out. It was a conflict that was not to have a lasting effect either on the GAA or Croke Park. When two years later the forces of nationalist Ireland embarked on violent revolution it was perhaps inevitable that the GAA and much of its membership would support the new movement. However, for a short period the mound of earth built up on the eastern side of the ground, where the Cusack Stand is today, became known as 'Hill 60' after a 60-metre-high hill fought over at the battle of Suvla Bay (part of this hill later became the more patriotically named Hill 16).

THE WAR OF INDEPENDENCE, BLOODY SUNDAY AND CIVIL WAR

After the 1916 Rising a number of events associated with the new revolutionary movement took place in Croke Park (this was somewhat of a U-turn in the policy that had previously banned the Irish Volunteers from drilling there). In October 1917 Sinn Féin held their convention in the Mansion House. In this political forum Eamon de Valera was elected president of the party. Once the political programme was decided the Irish Volunteers, the armed wing of the republican movement, went to Croke Park for their first convention since 1915. Over 1,000 attended. The rank and file sat in the uncovered stand while at a platform improvised from bales of hay sat de Valera, Cathal Brugha, Terence MacSwiney, Diarmid

Eamon de Valera, president of Sinn Féin, throws in the ball for a prisoners' dependants fund match at Croke Park in April 1919.

Lynch, Michael Collins and former Kerry football star Austin Stack. At this meeting these men were given the key posts that would pit them against the might of the British Empire – among the appointments were de Valera (President), Brugha (Chief of Staff) and Collins (Director of Intelligence).

In 1918 Joseph McGuinness, one of the first Sinn Féin MPs, successful in a by-election in South Longford, addressed a republican gathering in Croke Park. Among the other attractions was a Camogie match between Crokes and St Margaret's, Irish dancing, singing, recitations and refreshments 'at moderate prices'. Tickets were six pence and everyone was entered in a draw for P.H. Pearse's works in English. In May 1918 a Fenian commemoration was held at Croke Park.

Michael Collins throws in a sliotar to start a match at Croke Park.

Croke Park became a popular venue for matches to raise funds for the dependants of those detained by the British. Among these was a football match played on 6 April 1919 between Wexford and Tipperary. A handbill advertising the event read, 'You have heard of the suffering of Irishmen in gaols in Ireland. Do you know the anxiety of their dependants at home adds to their suffering? You can ease their anxiety in this matter by coming to the assistance of the Republican Prisoners' Dependants Fund … Will you come?'[8] Attending the match were de Valera, who threw in the ball, Arthur Griffith, the Lord Mayor of Dublin Lorcan Sherlock, Michael Collins and Arthur Griffith (Harry Boland was the referee). It was one of the last occasions on which the leaders of the republican movement were to be seen so blatantly in public. When the players walked onto the pitch St Laurence O'Toole's Pipe Band played 'The Wearin' of the Green'. When de Valera, the Lord Mayor and Alderman Nowlan, the President of the

From left, Michael Collins, Luke O'Toole and Harry Boland at Croke Park.

GAA, went to the middle of the pitch for the throw in at the start of the match the St James' Band played 'The Soldiers Song'.[9]

By late 1920 political and military events began to cause serious disruption to GAA fixures. Matches were intermittent and the numbers of spectators declined. At the end of October 1920, when Terence MacSwiney was nearing the end of his hunger strike and Kevin Barry was awaiting execution in Mountjoy Prison, the hurling semi-final was played between Dublin and Galway. It was a sombre occasion – 'At first glance the scene looked desolate – the new stand tenantless, and "Hill 60" opposite a big, bare, shapeless mound that told in eloquent ugliness the altered spirit of the occasion. Yet never did the playing pitch look fairer, the level sward catching an added depth of green from the tempered light of the autumn afternoon'.[10] In the following week all matches were cancelled as a mark of respect for the death of MacSwiney.

Kevin Moran

FORMER DUBLIN FOOTBALLER AND IRISH INTERNATIONAL SOCCER PLAYER

I had a great seat on my first visit to Croke Park, on my father's shoulders, for the 1963 All-Ireland football final between Dublin and Galway and Dublin won. I was seven years of age at the time and five years later I played my first game there and we won as well. It was only when I looked at the place from the pitch that I realised how huge it was with the stands towering over us. I played at midfield for James' Street CBC hurling team against Dún Laoghaire CBS in the Herald Cup final. I scored a few points and a goal that was really deflected into the net.

My first game for Dublin there was the semi-final of the National Football League of 1976 against Galway. Like the James' Street days I was at midfield and we went on to beat Kerry in the final. I liked the dressing rooms even though I was lucky to get a seat the first time I togged out for Dublin. A spot at the end of a long seat would be my ideal place and I sat there on my first visit as I was early. Soon Bobby Doyle came along and told me it was 'his place' and so I moved to another vacant site. Before long Paddy Reilly arrived with the same story – I was sitting in his place and so on. In the end Brian Mullins came over and caught me by the back of the neck and steered me to a seat near himself. That spot was mine then while I was a Dublin player.

A lot of people talk about the solo run I did in the early minutes of the All-Ireland final of that year against Kerry and think it was a planned tactic. That is not true – the whole field opened up in front of me and I just took off. I remember playing a one-two with Bernard Brogan that brought me very close to the Kerry goal but I never really looked up. I could have hopped the ball again and hand-passed it past Paudie O'Mahoney but instead I took a drop kick that went just wide. Even though the 1977 All-Ireland semi-final against Kerry is rated as one of the best games of all time the 1976 win will be number one with me forever. I was unknown as a Gaelic player in February and following a National League win in May we went on to beat Kerry in the All-Ireland final in September. The feeling was absolutely great because Dublin had a huge following and it was the first time in forty-two years that they had beaten Kerry in championship football.

Kerry beat us in the '78 final. It was my last game for Dublin and I will never forget the reaction when I walked into Old Trafford dressing room the following Tuesday. They couldn't believe the state of me. I was limping and had the 'remains' of a head bandage and the inside of the head was not great either after a few beers on Sunday night and Monday. They just broke down in laughter.

Croker is simply fantastic and it is hard to find its equal anywhere. The experience of playing major games in Croke Park was a big help to me in my soccer career – I never 'froze' in other big places as a result.

The Hill is the best part of Croke Park for me. When you are playing for Dublin and look at the sea of blue up there you realise you are playing in your own stadium. I always felt I was playing for them and there is no better feeling. I saw Dublin win the All-Ireland of 1974 from the Hill and I was there too in '75 when it was Kerry's day. The result was bad but I got onto the pitch after the game and that was a consolation.

With competitive matches suspended a headline in the *Sport* newspaper the following week announced 'Tipperary Challenges Dublin'. The challenge letter was published:

We understand that Tipperary's superiority over Dublin in football, despite two decisive victories by Tipperary, is being questioned by Dublin. We, therefore, challenge Dublin to a match on the first available date, on any venue and for any object.

Signed on behalf of the Tipperary football team.
T. Ryan, Sec.
E. O'Shea Capt.[11]

The match was set for Croke Park on 21 November 1920. There was significant interest because there were few matches being played at the time, the proceeds were going to 'an injured gael' and the match was a possible precursor to the All-Ireland final (Dublin had already qualified for the final while Tipperary were still in the badly interrupted Munster championship). A large crowd was confidently predicted.

The Tipperary team arrived in Dublin the night before the match. Their train journey was interrupted by a fracas with a group of British soldiers. When they arrived in Dublin they thought it best not to stay in Barry's Hotel as previously planned and they split up into small groups going to different hotels. Michael Hogan and Tommy Ryan, who were two of the Volunteers on the Tipperary team, heard that night that a 'big job' would come off the next day but were given no details. Elsewhere discussions took place between the Dublin Brigade of the IRA and the GAA about whether the match at Croke Park should be called off. The GAA decided not to cancel the game because it was felt if they did the British would associate the GAA with the morning's events.[12]

The events of what was to become known as Bloody Sunday, 21 November 1920, are generally regarded as having marked a decisive turning point in the military struggle between the British forces and those of the IRA, the military wing of the underground Dáil government. Three separate but connected events occurred on Bloody Sunday. First came the killings by Michael Collins' Squad of twelve British intelligence agents in their suburban homes in Dublin early in the morning. Two Royal Irish

Constabulary Auxiliary policemen were also killed. In the afternoon came the killing by British forces of fourteen civilians, including a Gaelic footballer Michael Hogan who was playing for Tipperary that day, at Croke Park. Finally, in the evening came the arrest and killing (in somewhat murky circumstances) of two high-ranking Dublin IRA officers, Brigadier Dick McKee and Vice Brigadier Peadar Clancy. In all, at least thirty people on both sides died in Dublin on that day within fifteen hours.

The official British version of events stated that the match at Croke Park had been arranged as cover for the assassinations of the secret service agents that morning. They had allegedly learned that a number of the men had made their way to Croke Park following the killings and it was their improbable intention that at Croke Park 'an officer would go to the centre of the field and, speaking from a megaphone, invite the assassins to come forward'.[13] This was not done. Sir Hamar Greenwood, Chief Secretary of Ireland, announced in the House of Commons that he regretted the deaths of innocent persons but stated that 'the responsibility rests with those who are a constant menace to all law-abiding persons in Ireland'.[14] Despite the official version of events the attack on Croke Park was certainly compatible with the unofficial British policy of reprisals in response to republican attacks – Balbriggan had been sacked in September and Cork city was burned in December as unofficial reprisals. The assertion was made by James Gleeson in his book, *Bloody Sunday*, that the Auxiliaries who had lost two of their comrades in the morning attacks tossed a coin to decide where they would wreak their vengeance. Would it be Croke Park or O'Connell Street?[15] Evidently Croke Park lost.

The Royal Irish Constabulary (RIC) contended that the first shots fired at Croke Park that morning were fired from the crowd before any Crown forces had entered. In a secret British military enquiry subsequent to the killings many of the RIC stated that when the first of their members got out of their lorries at the Royal Canal Bridge on Jones' Road a group of civilians standing at the start of the passage into the ground turned and ran at speed through the turnstiles. Some of the party, it was alleged, fired back in the direction of the Auxiliaries. This led to general gunfire. During the raid on Croke Park a total of 228 rounds of small arms ammunition were fired by the RIC and an Army machine gun at James' Avenue exit fired a total of 50 rounds (by all accounts these 50 shots were fired in the air to stop the crowd from leaving).

Contradicting the RIC were three members of the Dublin Metropolitan Police – an unarmed force who occupied a somewhat 'neutral' position during the conflict. Two of these DMP men were stationed on Jones' Road near the Canal Bridge. Neither reported seeing any civilians who could have threatened the Crown forces. One stated that shortly after 3.30pm about fifteen lorries of military and RIC arrived at the Canal Bridge entrance. The occupants of the first car ran down the passage leading to the football ground. He did not know who started the firing but reported that a military officer came running up to the bridge and said 'what is all the firing about, stop that firing'. The third DMP officer was on duty further down Jones' Road, outside the main entrance to Croke Park. He claims to have seen the 'smoking gun':

I was on duty outside the main entrance to Croke Park in Jones' Road. At about 3.25pm I saw six or seven large lorries accompanied by two armoured cars, one in front and one behind, pass along the Clonliffe Road from Drumcondra towards Ballybough. Immediately after a small armoured car came across Jones' Road from Fitzroy Avenue and pulled up at the entrance of the main gate. Immediately after that, three small Crossley lorries pulled up in Jones' Road. There were about ten or twelve men dressed in RIC uniforms in each. When they got out of the cars they started firing in the air which I thought was blank ammunition, and almost immediately firing started all round the ground.

One of those who admitted to firing on the crowd outlined his actions:

On November 21st 1920 I was in the second car of the convoy to Croke Park. The lorry halted just over the Canal Bridge. I saw no civilians on the bridge. There were some civilians in the passage leading to the turnstiles. I got out and went to the turnstiles as quickly as I could. As I got to the turnstiles I heard shots. I am certain they were revolver shots, a few shots fired quickly. They were fired inside the field. I tried to get through the turnstiles and found that they were locked. When getting over them a bullet hit the wall convenient to my head. This was the wall on the right hand side inside the archway and splinters of brick and mortar hit me in the face. It could not have been fired from outside the field. As I got inside I landed on my hands and feet. I saw young

Eileen Duffy O'Mahoney

FORMER DUBLIN CAMOGIE CAPTAIN AND GOALIE, AND WINNER
OF EIGHT ALL-IRELANDS

I have been going to Croke Park all my life and not just to Camogie games but to all sorts. I lived in Glasnevin and it was the regular thing to do on a Sunday – a few of us would go down and straight on to the Hill 16.

We had a nice past-time of picking a team to support on the spur of the moment and we would be cheering for that team right through the match. I remember giving an evening shouting for Roscommon and it was Meath other days because my mother was from Meath.

There was a magic about the Hill and you would get to know the different groups that came, all having their own favorite spots. We had the best fun in the world on the Hill.

The most famous regular patron when I was young was a person that everyone knew as 'The Lady With The Umbrella'. She always brought the brolly with her and like all of us picked her team and cheered them along. For the sake of sport some lads would support the other team and argue with her. She never opened it up but carried it all the time. But she would never give in and I saw her hit a few lads with the umbrella one day.

I played with the Celtic Club and we had a very good team and won county finals in Croke Park. I will never forget my first time playing there for Dublin. I won my first All-Ireland in 1949 when we travelled to Tipperary and beat the home team but the first match in Croke Park was the final with Antrim in 1950. I remember coming into the dressing room near the old Hogan Stand and it was a wonderful feeling. Even though the crowd was not huge we got a big welcome onto the field and that made me feel great. When I used to be on the Hill I thought the pitch was as level as a carpet but as a goal-keeper I discovered to my cost one day that it was far from even. I decided to stand firm and allow a ball to roll wide but before I knew anything it hit a tuft of grass and bounced in past me.

I loved playing in goal because I was fast on my feet and often raced out to the corner to get to the ball ahead of forwards. That worked great for me in my last final when we beat Antrim in 1957. When I was out of the goal the full-back Doretta Blackton always stepped back to the line just in case anything went wrong. I have fine memories of Croke Park where I won seven of my eight All-Ireland medals in the company of outfield players who prided their skill.

men aged between twenty and twenty-five running, stooping among the crowd, away from me between the fence and the wall. I pursued and discharged my revolver in their direction. My duties were identification of persons. I was in plain clothes having a Glengarry cap in my pocket for identification by my own men if necessary. Having been fired at I used my own discretion in returning fire. I aimed at individual young men who were running away trying to conceal themselves in the crowd. I used a .450 revolver and service ammunition. I chased them across the ground nearly to the wall on the East side. I then saw that a number of people were going back towards the main gate by which I came in. I rushed to that gate and took up my position outside to try and carry out my duties of identification. I stayed there until the ground was cleared, that is about an hour and a half.[16]

Inside the ground the scene was one of understandable panic. The match had started only a few minutes previously. Many noticed a military plane circle the grounds twice at low altitude. Most accounts agree that a few minutes later the firing began at the corner of the ground where the Grand Canal meets Jones' Road. People wondered afterwards if the aeroplane gave the signal for the firing. When the first shots rang out 'the great mass of people at that end of the ground swept like an avalanche on to the playing pitch. It was a terrifying scene. The firing increased; volley after volley rang out in quick succession'. Tommy Ryan, one of the Tipperary players, recalled that he ran toward the fence around the pitch, 'As I reached the paling, I saw one "Auxie" loading a round into the breech of his rifle who appeared to be looking in my direction. I dropped to the ground and a youngster near me fell, which I took to be from the shot that was intended for me.' Ryan escaped from Croke Park and found refuge in a house in Clonliffe road. The house was surrounded and he was captured. His shorts and shirt, which both had tricolours sewn into them, were torn off and he was walked naked back into Croke Park where he was put with the rest of the Tipperary team.[17] They expected that they would be shot. All of the crowd were searched before they left the ground; it was some hours before the ground was cleared. The last to be released were the Tipperary players. While they awaited their fate one of the team, Michael Hogan, lay dead at the north-east corner of the ground. However, a British military officer intervened, possibly saving the men the same fate suffered by Hogan.[18]

Fourteen innocent civilians were killed at Croke Park – John Scott, James Matthews, Jeremiah O'Leary, Patrick O'Dowd, Jane Boyle, William Robinson, Thomas Hogan, James Burke, Michael Feery, James Teehan, Joseph Traynor, Thomas Ryan, Michael Hogan and Daniel Carroll.

At this remove it is hard to imagine the terror of the day. But a sense of the tragedy can be gauged from the medical descriptions of the injuries received by the dead. The inquest on the death of Thomas Hogan by Dr Patrick Moran, of the Mater Hospital, stated:

Thomas Hogan was admitted to this Hospital at 4pm on November 21st. There was a small round wound 3/8 inch in diameter under the spine of the right scapula. There was a large round wound one inch in diameter just beneath the acromion process in front. This was apparently an exit wound. There were two other small wounds ¼ inch in diameter one inch above acromion process, and about an inch apart. These might have been caused by bone splinters. On admission the patient was bleeding profusely, and was in a state of severe collapse. The right arm was amputated on Monday, 22nd November. The shoulder joint was found to be completely disorganised. The head of the humerous was completely severed from the shaft and about two inches of the shaft was shattered. The auxillary border of the scapula was also shattered. A small piece of nickel casing was found in the region of the shoulder joint. Gas gangrene set in after the operation and the patient died at 12.30 on November 26th. Death was in my opinion due to toxaemia following gas gangrene following gunshot wounds.[19]

One of the youngest of the dead was schoolboy John Scott aged fourteen, from 16 Fitzroy Avenue, Drumcondra. He received a chest wound and was taken into the house of Mrs Coleman, 37 James' Avenue. Bleeding heavily, 'he was placed on a table. Mrs Coleman and her two little girls knelt down by his side and said some prayers, and the little boy made the responses. All the time the rattle of shots was heard outside and they were unable to get out for a drink of water for the dying child. He was suffering greatly and moaning a lot and died three-quarters of an hour later.'[20] Dr Monahan reported at the inquest:

In Scott I found on his back between 11th and 12th ribs about 1½ inches from middle line small circular wound apparently a bullet wound, and in front on left side a large ragged wound, roughly, triangular in outline measuring 1½ inches and extending from upper border of third to lower border of fourth rib, which was fractured. Probably in my opinion this was an exit wound. Death in my opinion due to shock and haemorrhage.

The body of John Scott was identified by his father.

Jane Boyle, twenty six years old and resident at 12 Lennox Street, Dublin, was the only woman killed on Bloody Sunday. She was employed in a Dublin butchers shop and was due to be married on the following Wednesday. She was admitted to the Mater Hospital on the evening of 21 November. She was dead on admission. The hospital's house surgeon, Dr Monahan, examined the body. He reported that he found a 'small bruise over left eye, her lower jaw was fractured on left side just below the angle. Her right clavicle and one or two upper ribs were also fractured. There was a circular wound on her back about 2½ inches from middle line on right side and between the ninth and tenth ribs. This was a bullet wound in my opinion. Death in my opinion was due to shock and haemorrhage'.

The best known of the killed was Michael Hogan, one of the Tipperary players. Hogan was later to be immortalised when the main stand at Croke Park was named after him. He was an Irish Volunteer and was playing full-back that day for Tipperary. According to Dr Cassin, when Hogan was brought to Jervis Street hospital that evening, 'life was then extinct'. He then carried out a post mortem;

… and found externally three wounds on left side of back, one circular about an inch in diameter, one longitudinal about one inch

Michael Hogan, the Tipperary player killed at Croke Park on Bloody Sunday.

Relatives of the Bloody Sunday dead and injured outside Jervis Street hospital during the military enquiry.

long, leading towards axilla, the other a small puncture wound not deep, on opening chest I found about one pint blood in left cavity. The fifth rib was shattered close to the circular wound. Left lung perforated through from a point corresponding to shattered rib at its apex. In the left cervical dome I found a small hole leading up into the neck, following this up I found a bullet ... in left lobe of Thyroid Gland. Death in my opinion was due to shock and haemorrhage following the injuries described.[21]

That night Croke Park, still damp with the blood of those who had been killed and injured, was littered with 'overcoats, umbrellas, walking sticks, hats, caps, ladies jewellery, etc. as well as about 200 bicycles. Evidently getting news of this, a mob swept down on the park and rushed the gates. The few officials were helpless and could do nothing to prevent the wholesale looting that followed. Women, girls and young men, carried away handfuls of coats'.[22]

On Tuesday night Hogan's body was removed from Jervis Street Hospital to the Pro-Cathedral. The cortège included the rest of the

An eerie scene. The view when looking towards what is now Hill 16 at Croke Park, the day after Bloody Sunday.

Tipperary team. After morning mass the remains of Hogan were taken by train for burial in Grangemockler, Tipperary. Unlike the pomp and ceremony that attended the funeral service for the dead British agents at Westminster Cathedral in London, the funerals of the Irish victims were muted. On Thursday 25 November six of the victims of the 'Croke Park horror' were buried in Glasnevin. Due to military restrictions the cortèges were limited to friends, relatives and neighbours. There were no emblems displayed at the funerals. As the procession passed through the streets people respectfully saluted.[23]

Within a couple of weeks of the tragic events of 21 November 1920 Croke Park was again being used for club matches. However, it was not until after the Truce in July 1921 that an inter-county match was played at what was now known as 'headquarters'. The match was an All-Ireland football final between Louth and Dublin. The crowd was not as large as would have been expected before the war but the atmosphere was reminiscent of more carefree days – 'the rival war cries were indeed a welcome break in the restraint and silence that have prevailed so long'.[24] In December 1921, just before the signing of the Anglo-Irish Treaty, the final of the Croke Park Tournament was at last played (Dublin beat Mayo).

After the signing of the Anglo-Irish Treaty, which ended the War of Independence, the first inter-county match at Croke Park was played on 26 February 1922. It was a fundraiser for the Prisoners' Dependants Fund between Tipperary and Kildare. An advertisement for the match urged the reader to 'Be one of the Crowd! The Cause is Good!! And the Game Will be Extra!!!'[25] Another ad read, with surprising insensitivity to those who had lost loved ones on Bloody Sunday, 'Desperate Shooting at Croke Park (for goals and points)', 'Republicans, Free Staters and Separatists (Sinn Féiners All!!) adjourn to the old venue for a few hours relaxation'.[26] Alderman Mrs Tom Clarke, widow of the executed 1916 leader, threw in the ball after having her photograph taken with soldiers injured during the recent conflict.[27]

Such shows of nationalist unity at Croke Park were soon to be a thing of the past. By May the widening division between pro- and anti-Treaty sides had become evident at matches and it was necessary for the GAA to issue warnings to those attending the All-Ireland football semi-final that 'political literature of any kind whatsoever will not be allowed to be either distributed or sold on the grounds'.[28] In the following month Dublin and Tipperary, who had played at Croke Park on Bloody Sunday, met in the delayed 1920 All-Ireland. War of Independence hero Dan Breen threw in the ball in front of 25,000 spectators. Fittingly Tipperary won. After the match the players went to the spot where Hogan was killed (the corner of the ground where the Cusack Stand and Hill 16 meet today). A small number of the crowd stayed to join in the tribute. According to a press report the C.J. Kickham Band 'played the mournful strains of the "Dead March", the crowd stood bareheaded in silence and when the music ceased all knelt in prayer on the scene of the grim tragedy'.[29]

By the end of June the comradeship of the previous years was shattered by the outbreak of Civil War. The conflict threw the championship into chaos once again – a chaos exacerbated by a railway strike. The big-day atmosphere at Croke Park did not return until the autumn when the 1921 championship was resumed. On 1 October 1922 Kildare played Dublin in a Leinster football semi-final. A sign of the times was that the following week at Newbridge Internment Camp the prisoners of Dublin took on those of Kildare.[30] On 4 March 1923 the 1921 hurling final was played between Limerick and Dublin. The match was notable for the first presentation of a 'handsome challenge cup' that was donated by Liam MacCarthy (a well-known GAA man in London who had been president of the London GAA for four years). In addition to the first presentation of the MacCarthy trophy the match was also notable for the new political elite that occupied the VIP section in the stand. President Cosgrave was

Micheál Ó Sé

RADIO NA GAELTACHTA

WINNER OF ALL-IRELAND MEDALS WITH KERRY IN 1969 AND 1970

Is cuimhin liom imirt i bPáirc An Chrócaigh don gcéad uair I gCluiche Ceannais na gColáisti idir St Brendan's ó Chill Áirne agus Naomh Mel ó Longfort sa bhliain 1963. Bhíos ag imirt sa chúinne mar chosantóir le Brendan's agus cé bhí anuas orm ach Jimmy Hanniffy – imreoir nótalta ar feadh blianta in a dhiaidh sin.

Theip orainn agus dúrt liom fhéin go mba bhreá filleadh agus imirt ann le Ciarraí uair éigin. Bhí an t-ádh orm – tharla sé agus bhaineas dhá All-Ireland ann le Ciarraí.

Bhí sé go h-aoibhinn ar fad – sluaite móra – bannaí ceoil – ard atmasféar – agus mo chomharsain féin ó Árd Na Caithne ag liúriagh agus mé ag dreapadh na gcéimeanna ar an Hogan agus an Corn á bhronnadh.

Bhí filíocht á chumadh acu. A dhuine, ach níorbh aon iontas é – nach raibh cuid acu gaolmhar leis An Spailpín, file mór 'Mherica a rugadh in Árd Na Caithne. Níl áit mar Pháirc An Chrócaigh sa tsaol seo.

I remember playing in Croke Park for the first time in the All-Ireland Colleges Final between St Brendan's from Killarney and St Mel's from Longford in 1963. I was playing corner back and who was marking me but Jimmy Hanniffy – a prominent player for many years after that.

We lost and I said to myself it would be grand to return and play there with Kerry.

I was lucky – it happened and I won two All-Irelands there with Kerry.

It was wonderful – big crowds, bands, super atmosphere – and my own neighbours from Árd na Caithne applauding as I went up the steps of the Hogan Stand to accept the cup.

They were composing poetry. Man, it was no wonder – weren't some of them related to An Spailpín, a famous poet in America who was born in Árd na Caithne. There's no place in this world like Croke Park.

joined by Joseph McGrath, Ernest Blythe and Eamon Duggan and the ball was thrown in by the neutral figure of Joseph O'Mara of the O'Mara Opera Company. Also attending the match were a group of students from Trinity College hoping to pick up a few tips or inspiration before their historic first match against University College Dublin.[31] By the end of 1923 the GAA was beginning to clear the backlog of matches. The hurling final for 1922 featuring Kilkenny and Tipperary played on 9 September drew a crowd of 26,119 and took in a gate of £2,403. In October Dublin beat Galway in the football final.

FÊTE, 'TAILTEANN' GAMES AND RODEO

In June 1923 Croke Park was transformed into a 'pleasure ground' for a two-week fête organised by Central Council to clear the debt from the Croke Park improvements.[32] At the opening ceremony Dan McCarthy, GAA President, addressed the crowd with a megaphone – 'the novel operations of the instrument were regarded with much interest'. In his speech he said that the GAA 'wanted to have Croke Park so well equipped that our representatives on the Olympic Council may be able in the near future to suggest that the great games should be held in the Irish capital'.[33] Hurling, football, camogie and rounders competitions were organised. In addition there were Irish dancing, band promenades, concerts, a *ceilidh* ball as well as 'chairoplant, hobby horses, Brooklyn Cake Walk, mountain slide and swingboats'. One specially advertised event was a wireless exhibition when people could listen to broadcasts from stations 'hundreds of miles away'.[34]

In August 1924 one of the most important events to take place in the new Free State was the holding of the *Tailteann* Games. The idea of reviving the ancient Celtic games established by King Lugh in honour of his foster-mother Tailte in the seventh century BC was first mooted in the 1880s. In October 1921 in the last days of the War of Independence a discussion took place between several members of Dáil Éireann during which de Valera said that a gathering of the Irish race would be held in Dublin or Paris (if the peace negotiations in London had failed). J.J. Walsh, soon to be Postmaster General of the new Irish State, was asked to organise the event and in February of the following year a General Council

Mick O'Dwyer

FORMER KERRY FOOTBALL PLAYER, KERRY FOOTBALL MANAGER,
KILDARE FOOTBALL MANGER, NOW MANAGER OF LAOIS

My first trip to Croke Park was for the All-Ireland football final of 1953 between Kerry and Armagh. Myself and Eric Murphy travelled through the night on the Ghost Train from Cahirsiveen and arrived into Kingsbridge Station in the early hours of Sunday morning. The train was packed and we all walked into town and stayed on O'Connell Street until the Pillar Café opened. We had a fine big breakfast then and stayed around for a while before going up to Croke Park.

We arrived very early to get a good look at the place we had heard so much about and it looked even better. I watched the match from the Canal End and had a great view of Bill McCorry's penalty kick that went wide. I tried to take everything in and my greatest memory is of Armagh's midfielder Malachy McEvoy storming down the field on a mighty solo run. I can 'see' a few of Tadhgie Lyne's long-range points as well. It was great to see Kerry win on my first trip to the famous place.

Five months later I was back and I played there for the first time. It happened in a roundabout way. Billy Huggard of the Butler Arms Hotel in Waterville was a friend of Paddy O'Keeffe who was the General Secretary of the GAA at the time. They arranged a match between Waterville and a Malahide selection to take place after a National League game between Dublin and Roscommon. I played on the 40 with Billy on the wing and we won by a point. It was a great feeling to score a goal and a point at the Railway end of the field near Hill 16. I thought the sod was lovely to run and play on but I was surprised to find out that it had a lot of little humps and hollows.

It is now fifty years since I played that match and I have been back regularly. In the early days I went there if I was in Dublin for a weekend and standing under the Cusack Stand was my favourite perch. It was a great honour to play in ten All-Ireland finals and to manage Kerry in ten more finals. I have great memories of the place with Kildare and winning two Leinster titles and reaching the All-Ireland final of 1998. And then there was Laois in 2003 with the county's first Leinster title since 1946. Croke Park is some sight on a big day – you wouldn't get the likes of it anywhere.

and a number of sub-committees were set up and began to hold weekly meetings. While the GAA played a significant role in the games the committees were made up of representatives from a number of other organisations including the Gaelic League, the Camogie Association and the governing bodies of athletics, boxing, swimming, rowing, handball, chess, archery as well as representatives from music, Irish dancing, drama and literature. The games were scheduled for 6–13 August 1922. However, when the Civil War broke out the games faced postponement. The American delegation, by far the most important for the success of the games, wrote a telegram in July informing the organisers that they would not attend the games; 'Fighting in Dublin cause; public against touching Games under circumstances; peace will revive American sentiment, ensuring full team'. The organisers bowed to the inevitable and postponed the games.[35]

In October 1923 as the Civil War was drawing to an end the games were revived and the country geared up for the event. The importance of the games went beyond mere sports. The *Tailteann* Games was the first occasion during which the fledgling nation was able to show the world its abilities. Competitors came from Ireland, England, Scotland, Canada, Wales, the USA, South Africa and Australia. Showcasing the organising

Irish wolfhounds and celtic warriors, symbols of a great Gaelic past, prepare to enter Croke Park at the opening of the 1924 *Tailteann* Games.

Tadgh De Brún

RTÉ CAMERAMAN

I have worked on seventy-seven All-Ireland finals for RTÉ and, like everything else in Croke Park, match coverage has changed dramatically during the years. In the early years live coverage began just a few minutes before the throw-in and ended with the presentation of the Cup. Nowadays All-Ireland final television coverage lasts for five and a half hours.

In the early years coverage was very basic – two cameras in the Upper Hogan Stand and one down in the central tunnel. The next stage of development was the placing of a camera on a scaffold behind each goal. By the late 1970s, RTÉ had come to the point of being able to place cameras outside the doors of the dressing rooms under the old Cusack Stand to catch the teams heading for the green patch above. As the teams came down the tunnel for the 1977 football final between Dublin and Armagh I remember Pat O'Neill, the Dublin half-back, stopping and shaking hands with me while wishing me well at the same time. He had no recollection of it when I mentioned it to him at the victory banquet later that night.

The next innovation was a camera in the winner's dressing room and that guaranteed utter chaos. The number of followers who got into the dressing room then was phenomenal. That the late Mick Dunne managed to conduct interviews among the heaving masses remains a mystery, but it always worked. I have seen many winning dressing rooms down the years but the Tyrone one of 2003 was unique. The sight of the entire team, arm in arm, singing the National Anthem was truly memorable, and that was after the match.

On one occasion at Croke Park after a Kilkenny victory I tried to line up Fan Larkin for an interview but there was reluctance on his part. He then declined and apologised before stating that he was in a hurry. I noticed he was still wearing his Kilkenny jersey and socks even though shoes, trousers and jacket were now in place. He left in an awful hurry. I learned later that he was heading for the half-five Mass in Gardiner Street Church.

The 1980s were not too old by the time we had our own studio high up near the roof of the Nally Stand. Access was via a high and very shaky ladder. Now the new Croke Park has brought us state of the art facilities and we travel to the studio by an elevator to the sixth floor. For me all has changed … except one thing. Joe Rock always appears with a cup of tea for me in the tunnel on All-Ireland final day.

ᴀonᴀᴄ́ ᴄᴀiᴌᴄéᴀnn
FROM 2—18 AUGUST

GRAND
OPENING CEREMONY
AT CROKE PARK
Saturday, 2nd August, commencing at 3 p.m.

PROGRAMME

OFFICIAL RECEPTION AND MARCH PAST OF COMPETITORS AND OPENING OF GAMES.

International Shinty-Hurling Contest: SCOTLAND v. IRELAND

Gymnastic Display: ARTANE INDUSTRIAL SCHOOL.

SUNDAY, 3rd AUGUST.
3 p.m.—Ireland v. America. International Hurling. Croke Park.
4 p.m.—Ireland v. England. International Camogie. Bray.
4.30 p.m.—Ulster v. Munster. National Football. Croke Park.
7 p.m.—Ireland v. England. International Football. Croke Park.

MONDAY, 4th AUGUST
3 p.m.—Connaught v. Leinster. National Football. Croke Park.
4.15 p.m.—Ireland v. England. International Hurling. Croke Park.

TUESDAY, 5th AUGUST.
7 p.m.—England v. America. International Hurling. Croke Park.

WEDNESDAY, 6th AUGUST.
7 p.m.—England v. Wales. International Hurling. Croke Park.

THURSDAY, 7th AUGUST.
7 p.m.—England v. Scotland. International Hurling. Croke Park.

FRIDAY, 8th AUGUST.
3 p.m.—Scotland v. America. International Hurling. Croke Park.
7 p.m.—Ireland v. Wales. International Hurling. Croke Park.

SATURDAY, 9th AUGUST.
2.30 p.m.—Ireland v. Scotland. International Hurling. Croke Park.
4 0 p.m.—Wales v. America. International Hurling. Croke Park.

SUNDAY, 10th AUGUST.
2.30 p.m.—Connaught v. Leinster. Hurling. Croke Park.
3.45 p.m.—National Football Final. Croke Park.

WEDNESDAY, 13th AUGUST.
2.30 p.m.—International Athletics and Cycling. Croke Park.

THURSDAY, 14th AUGUST.
2.30 p.m.—International Athletics and Cycling. Croke Park.

FRIDAY, 15th AUGUST.
2.30 p.m.—International Athletics and Cycling. Croke Park.

SATURDAY, 16th AUGUST.
2.30 p.m.—International Athletics and Cycling Finals. Croke Park.

SUNDAY, 17th AUGUST.
2 p.m.—National Hurling Final. Croke Park.

HANDBALL EVENTS AT BALLYMUN AND CLONDALKIN.

For full details and particulars of all items see Official Daily Programme and Syllabus on Sale during Games.

Visitors Accomodation Bureau, 105 Middle Abbey Street,

ADMISSION 1/- & 2/-   Grand Stand (Reserved) 5/-

Season Ticket, £1 1s. 0d., each admitting to the General Enclosures AT ALL OUTDOOR EVENTS; can be had from the following: Messrs. Clerys, Crottys, Elverys, Helys, Leslies, or at the Central Office, 5a College Street, Dublin.

abilities of the new state, it was also a showcase for an early tourism industry. Politically it attempted to show that the Irish race was an ancient one that had for centuries been suppressed by a foreign power. Now that the yoke of foreign domination had been cast aside the greatness of the Irish race would once again shine.

Croke Park was central to the success of the games. The opening and closing ceremonies were to be held there and although the *Tailteann* Games included many events not held at Croke Park such as golf, gymnastics, rowing, literature, motor boat racing, motor cycling, swimming, pipe band, singing, tennis, tug o' war, yachting, stained glass, landscape and seascape painting, it was at the Jones' Road ground that most of the popular events would be held. However, despite the improvements that had been made to Croke Park since it was bought from Dineen it was a long way from being a world-class venue.

In January 1924 in an article written by 'Celt', the question was asked 'Is Croke Park a Suitable Arena for High-class Contests?'. Celt contended that those who had used the grounds for athletics and cycling had long complained about its facilities but to no avail. Indeed there

A newspaper advertisement for the 1924 *Tailteann* Games.

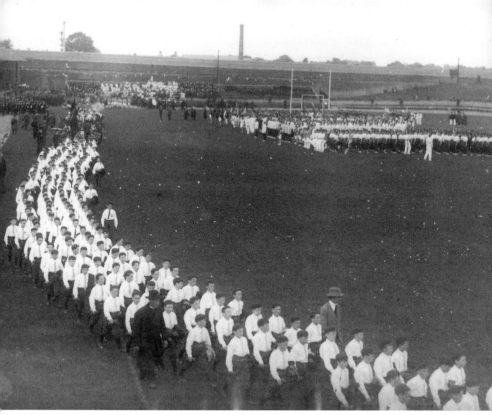

Children parading at the opening ceremony of the *Tailteann* Games 1924.

were numerous grounds for criticism. There was no cinder track, the running tracks were badly laid with irregular bends – one of which was 'positively dangerous', the banking of the cycle track was 'haphazard and imperfect' while as a jumping arena the ground was 'notoriously unpopular'. In addition the facilities for spectators were poor with stands for about 9,000 people and 'precarious footholds for the rest'. The article concluded ominously 'Just imagine the famous band of the 69th Regiment coming all the way from New York to lead our exiled champions, fresh, let us hope, from their Paris Olympiad triumphs, on to such a ground as Croke Park'.[36] The *Tailteann* Committee took action and, with the help of a government loan of £7,500, set about improving the facilities including the running track.[37]

The games opened on 2 August at 3 p.m. at Croke Park. It was a hugely successful day. One report enthused that the opening ceremony 'was one of the finest things ever witnessed in the city. Nothing of the kind had ever been attempted before, not even on a small scale, and few believed that Saturday's ceremonial, or anything approaching it, from the spectator point

A fireworks display at the end of the 1924 *Tailteann* Games.

of view, was possible'. The city was bedecked with bunting, festoons, plants and flowers. Croke Park had been transformed for the event. A mock castle and round tower forming the entrance to the ground and other ancient symbols tempted the visitor to imagine they were travelling back to a golden era of Irish history. Overhead an airplane display took place. From the grounds of Clonliffe College there was an Irish army artillery salvo while sirens from ships in Dublin Bay competed with the pealing of bells throughout the city. At one end of the ground a 500-strong choir sang a welcome to the athletes and spectators. It was indeed an auspicious occasion. With the formalities over the first event of the games, a shinty match between Ireland and Scotland, began. With everyone dressed to the nines, one reporter commented 'we do not often have silk-hats at a hurling match'.[38]

Over the next two weeks Croke Park hosted the hurling, football, athletics and cycling competitions. There was a significant foreign contingent. With the Paris Olympics just over many newly-crowned Olympians competed at Croke Park. The world-class American and Canadian athletes dominated the sprint events. In the high jump American Olympic gold medal winner Harold Osborn was pushed by Kildare footballer Larry Stanley who had no high jump coaching. It was an epic contest that has gone down in the history of Irish athletics. Despite

COWGIRLS TRICK RIDING

This was one of the most popular events at the Wembley Rodeo. The winner of the World's Championship Trick Riding Contest for Cowgirls, Miss Vera McGinnis, is an Irish-American. She will defend her title at

Dublin's First

RODEO

Championship Exhibition of Cowboy Sports at

CROKE PARK, August 18 to 25

Twice daily, 2.30 and 6.30 p.m.   LEON D. BRITTON, Manager

Learn what "at home on a horse" really means.

Book your seats now at Leslies Ltd. 116 Grafton Street. No extra charge for advance booking. Country residents should book at once by post. Tickets, 10s 6d, and 8s. 6d.

Above: Cowboys and indians at Croke Park during the 1924 Rodeo.

Left: The advertisement for the Croke Park Rodeo of August 1924.

Stanley's personal best of six feet two inches Osborn won the *Tailteann* gold. The 1,000 metre cycling was won by the great Bertie Donnelly who went on to dominate Irish cycling for decades (his bicycle has been loaned to the GAA Museum in Croke Park). In all over 78,000 people watched the *Tailteann* events.

The *Tailteann* Games were staged on two more occasions, in 1928 and 1932. The 1928 games were on a smaller scale than the first one but it was successful nonetheless. Many athletes who had competed at the Amsterdam Olympics again made the trip to Dublin. Among them were Ireland's hammer Olympic champion, Dr Pat Callaghan, Canada's sprint medallist, Phil Edwards, and again Harold Osborn. In 1932 there were a number of difficulties. These games were also the last to be held. With the Olympics in Los Angeles, the proximity of the Eucharistic Congress in Dublin and the lack of enthusiasm by An Taoiseach Eamon de Valera, these games were the least successful.

Apart from the *Tailteann* Games, Croke Park was the most important venue for Irish athletics. Until the mid-1930s Croke Park hosted many great athletics events. In addition to the Irish championships, international matches (against Scotland and France) and 'Open' meetings (organised by Clonliffe Harriers and by various trade unions including the Drapers, Dublin Police and Printers Unions) were organised. Large crowds attended these meets and star names often competed. In September 1926 Otto Pelzer of Germany broke the world record for the 1500 metres in Croke Park.

Almost as soon as the 1924 *Tailteann* Games ended one of the most unusual events ever held at Croke Park began. It was a rodeo held during the week of 18–25 August 1924. One popular event was the amateur bucking horse competition when volunteers from the audience competed for a £5 prize. The winner was the one who stayed on longest but the money was only handed over if the rider lasted for more than thirty seconds. Among those who won was Jack Crotty of the Curragh who lasted for thirty-two seconds. Others, like Percival Walker of Raheny, were less successful. He 'was thrown immediately on entering the arena and had to be removed on a stretcher, though not seriously injured'.[39] Another popular event was steer wrestling when cowboys on horseback lassoed calves and then brought them to ground and bound their legs. There was 'great delight' when the Irish calves managed to elude their American pursuers –

The United States hurling team parade at the
1928 *Tailteann* Games opening ceremony.

The opening of the 1932 *Tailteann* Games at Croke Park.

'the calves, showing uncanny intelligence, dodged, twisted, and turned, cleverly anticipating the twirling rope amidst great applause'.[40] The rodeo was a huge success. The festival of the skills of the American west attracted up to 20,000 people each day for the matinée and evening shows (excursion trains ran from different parts of the country every day). However, some begrudgers were unimpressed by the spectacle and one declared that he 'had seen as good at Hengler's Circus at the Rotunda in the old days'.[41]

CHAPTER THREE

1925-1946

1931 All-Ireland hurling final between Cork and Kilkenny.

The 1920s was an important decade for the GAA. It was one in which it not only survived the ravages of Civil War and helped to heal the divisions caused by the conflict, it also managed to expand successfully. This period saw the introduction of under-eighteen competitions, the National Hurling and Football Leagues and the inter-provincial Railway Cup competitions. The success and growth of the Association had once led to the demand for a national stadium. It now led to a demand that each county have its own stadium. When William P. Clifford became President of the GAA in 1926 one of his first proposals was that each county should buy its own grounds.[1] The shining example for all was headquarters – 'the sight of Croke Park set visiting Gaels asking themselves the question why every county should not have a Croke Park of its own on a more modest scale'.[2]

In 1924 only Croke Park and Austin Stack Park in Tralee were owned by the GAA.[3] At the same time only a handful of grounds were devoted

Runners competing in an athletics event in Croke Park in the 1920s, possibly organised by the Clonliffe Harriers.

exclusively to Gaelic games. One notorious case in point was Market's Field, Limerick, which was used for rugby on a Saturday and the GAA often competed with a circus, a horse-jumping competition or another sports meeting to use it on Sunday. In the campaign for the purchase of grounds the provincial councils encouraged the county boards to find suitable sites and raise a percentage of the capital that was then supplemented by funds from the provincial council. In one year in the 1920s the Leinster council invested £4,400 and Munster council £2,250.[4] Within the space of two decades there was a nationwide network of GAA-owned county grounds. Two of the later purchases were the Limerick Gaelic Grounds in 1938 and Fitzgerald Park, Killarney, in 1945.[5] But at all times Croke Park remained the Association's most important venue. In 1924 it held its Annual Congress there for the first time and at the 1925 Annual Congress it was officially decided that Croke Park would be the venue for all future All-Ireland finals.

During the Civil War the GAA managed to avoid the deep divisions caused by the conflict. Once it was over the GAA soon became a pillar of

Croke Park in the mid 1920s with the Long Stand (to the left) and the original Hogan Stand.

the new independent Ireland. If the Abbey Theatre represented the higher end of the Irish cultural landscape, Croke Park, as a manifestation of the GAA, became the most popular feature. Of course, the GAA and Croke Park were not within everyone's interests but Croke Park was a place where the Irish community could gather in communal celebration in a way that was not possible elsewhere. As a result Croke Park was where the leaders of the state paraded themselves every September. Although on any All-Ireland day each political party could have raised a quorum at the ground, the best seats at Croke Park were reserved for the current political elite. First the Cumann na Gael government populated the best seats of the VIP section, then in 1932 came Fianna Fáil under de Valera. Rows of government ministers accompanied their leaders. And so it continues even today. But it was not just the secular leaders who were prominent. One of the recurrent Croke Park images was of a bishop or archbishop throwing in the ball or sliotar. One of the first recorded occasions was in 1928 when the Most Reverend Dr Cullen, Bishop of Kildare and Leighlin, threw in the ball. In the next couple of years the Most Reverand Dr Hayden, Archbishop of Hobart and the Bishop of Zanzibar joined local figures like the Archbishop of Cashel and the Bishop of Ossary at the centre of the field. As patron of the Association the Bishop of Cashel and Emly normally did the honours. This ceremony only ended in the late 1970s.

Some of the small details of Croke Park that we now take for granted were introduced at this time. In the 1925 hurling final a 'recording board' was erected at one end of the ground to show the team's scores.[6] The boys from the Artane industrial school band were becoming an annual feature.

They entertained the crowd before the big games by playing popular tunes or giving gymnastic displays. Prior to the start of the replay of the 1926 football final 'The Soldiers Song' was played (by the Garda Síochána Band) for the first time with 'many persons jumping to their feet and uncovering'.[7] In 1925 it was decided that the 1,400-seat stand erected for the *Tailteann* Games should be named after the Tipperary player killed on Bloody Sunday.[8] On 17 March 1926 it was officially named the Hogan Stand at an 'Irish Ireland' celebration with Irish dancing, a gymnastic display by the Artane Boys and a football match between Tipperary and Dublin – a replay of the unfinished 1920 game. The plaque to Hogan was unveiled by P.D. Breen, President of the GAA, in front of Ernest Blythe, Minister for Finance, J.J. Walsh, Minister for Posts and Telegraphs, Eoin O'Duffy, Chief Commissioner, Garda Síochána and Major-General D.

An early photograph of the Artane Boys Band.

Hogan, GOC Eastern Command and the brother of the man being honoured. While there was no official decision to change the name of the hill and no naming ceremony the name Hill 60 was eventually transformed into the more patriotic 'Hill 16'. This change came about gradually and it was not until the 1930s that this area of the ground became universally referred to as Hill 16 in honour of the 1916 Rising, rather than Hill 60 after a World War One battle. The change was later given a degree of dubious historical credence when it was asserted that the hill had been formed out of the rubble of the 1916 Rising. This flew in the face of the fact that it had been formed in 1915 and therefore could not have been constructed out of the ruins of the following year's rebellion.

FIRST RADIO BROADCAST

In 1926 a new era in Irish sport began when the All-Ireland hurling semi-final between Kilkenny and Galway was broadcast to radio listeners. The significance of the press in promoting the game had first been given recognition in 1925 when a press table was fitted out at Croke Park. The Kilkenny-Galway game was a landmark broadcast as it was the first radio broadcast of a field game in Europe. That Croke Park and 2RN, the Irish radio station, hold this distinction can largely be attributed to a prohibition on the BBC from transmitting news and sports results before 7pm in order to protect newspaper sales.[9] The first voice of Gaelic games was P.D. Mehigan, the popular GAA journalist who wrote under the pen-name 'Carbery'. Mehigan was asked by P.S. O'Hegarty, Secretary of Posts and Telegraphs, to take part in the experiment. Arriving at Croke Park half an hour before the match he met the engineer and began to inspect the mysterious web of wires and cables that greeted him. Putting on the leather headset with brass tube to speak into he sat with only slips of paper with the team lists in front of him:

> The mysterious signal came that I was 'on the air', and the engineer nodded to 'fire away'. Without more ado I 'fired away' and found that I could spout freely enough, particularly as soon as the game, which I was so familiar with, started. At half-time I had to do a summary on the first half and so on to the end. I was very tired at the finish; they were beaming in the engineer's room below and tapped me on the back. They told me

★ Readers who intend to listen-in to the-broadcast of a running commentary on the Inter-Provincial matches on St. Patrick's Day (Commentator: Éamonn de Barra, Editor " An Gaedeal ") will find this diagram of assistance.

A plan of Croke Park in the 1930s, which appeared in papers to assist the increasing number of radio listeners to follow the action.

I had done fine; I didn't believe them. But I knew I was only a raw recruit and had a bit to learn. Yet I got a great kick out of it all, and was glad to help to spread the light, about the loved game of my childhood.[10]

The experiment was regarded as an immediate success and the Munster hurling final and its subsequent two replays were the next to be broadcast. The first broadcast of an All-Ireland was the 1926 football final between Kerry and Kildare. Reviewing this broadcast, the *Irish Radio Journal* wrote glowingly of the great future for sports broadcasting; 'the relay of sporting fixtures accomplished in this fashion make an irresistible appeal, and will of a certainty prove one of the most eagerly awaited features of the service'.[11]

HEADQUARTERS

It was during this period that Croke Park became a hallowed sporting ground. The main venue of the GAA since it was purchased in 1913 and with an intermittent association with the games since the 1895 championship, Croke Park now had its own history. This history provided

Action from an early camogie All-Ireland at Croke Park.

reference points against which days could be judged. After the 1926 football final one journalist wrote, 'In the history of Croke Park there are days fresh in the minds of all its patrons. None will forget the football struggle between Kerry and Louth that drew more than 30,000 people together a dozen years ago; or the superb display of hurling to which Kilkenny and Tipperary treated 28,000 spectators four years ago. But these events pale in comparison with the match of yesterday, with its breaking of all records, its unparalleled enthusiasm, its wild excitement.'[12] In a report on the second replay of the Cork-Kilkenny 1931 hurling All-Ireland one journalist wrote that the mention of Cork and Kilkenny 'fills the ground with heroic figures, too many of whom will never grace it, or earth, again. Surely it is heroic and historic ground; and it is because of its associations that any championship contested to finality there assumes a dignity and glamour which no other events I know of can pretend to claim. Can the players who will appear in this year's finals be wholly indifferent to the

An All Ireland junior football semi-final between Louth and Sligo in the 1920s.

feeling that they are pressing in the tracks of great champions and Gaels of other generations? The shades of these earlier protagonists of a virile race must haunt and hallow the scene of their triumphs.'[13] Another commented that Croke Park was 'a dreamland for me, an inner film upon which many emotions cast their outlines and many once loved figures pass in silent review'.[14] Yet another wrote of the 'Spirit of Croke Park' and of how sitting in the Hogan Stand 'watching the thousands and listening to the parading pipe bands, one thought of the changes 40 years had wrought; of the evolution of this Croke Park itself, and of how closely it was associated with the fortunes of the Irish Nation ... Here was the heart and soul of Ireland which had seen a great awakening'.[15]

On a more fundamental and basic level the Croke Park we know today began to emerge. The unique atmosphere that sets Croke Park out from other sports stadiums developed in the 1920s and 1930s. The All-Ireland finals at Croke Park became not just a matter that concerned the counties

The start of the 1924 All-Ireland junior football final between London and Westmeath with Hill 60 in the background.

who were playing. They became national affairs with interest and spectators spreading far beyond the confines of the two competing counties. The high number of women attending the games, the healthy rivalry between supporters and the personal knowledge of the supporters with the players on the field helped create this atmosphere that, to a large extent, remains unchanged today.

As the crowds became larger they generated their own interest. Framing the action on the field their presence, and size, gave a match much more importance. The sea of faces and the collective roar had become a central part of the occasion. A Croke Park patron wrote, 'Who can put into words the feelings of an old Gael when he sees around him on All-Ireland Final Day the scores of thousands from the four corners of this little country and the wave of pride which must come uppermost when he thinks that he had done his little bit to make such a place and such a day possible'.[16] Often the newspaper headline the day after a match was not about the actual match but about the number of people who watched it while a common front-page photograph was not of the players but of the sea of faces in the stands and terraces of Croke Park. Reading a write-up of the minutes that preceded the start of the 1931 hurling final between Cork and Kilkenny, one cannot fail to be struck by the similarity of the occasion with a final of today and agree with the author's final sentiments:

> Then on to the pitch in their brown kilts and green jackets, their heads thrown back and their saffron cloaks flying, came the Volunteer Pipers from Cork. The crowd began to cheer. Next the Kilkenny Band, in their green kilts and crimson cloaks, marching grimly determined. Round the field they went, their shrill wild music heating the blood of the crowd, rousing the imagination to cope with the great deeds to come. A ripple of anticipation came over the throng. Here they were, these contestants who twice before had fought that close battle in which neither side yielded the fraction of an inch, but today must decide the issue … No sooner were we seated than the Artane Band broke into the 'Soldiers Song' and again we were on our feet … It was one of the few really native scenes that I have seen in my own country. And if you looked at the crowd on every side you could recognise everywhere the strong, unchiselled faces which are the distinctly Celtic type. You saw them again on most of the players on the field. As a piece of local colour, the thing was magnificent. One would like the whole world to have seen it.[17]

Of course the most important part of the day came once the match had begun. The 1920s and 1930s was an era rich in great games, great teams and great players. It was the time when the interest in any game went beyond those of the counties involved. It was the beginning of the GAA's collective memory – a body of folklore for all those with an interest in the games.

Football emerged as the most popular sport in Ireland in the 1920s. In part this was due to the revival of the 1903 clashes between Kerry and Kildare that had been so instrumental in originally increasing the popularity of the games. Kildare, wearing the all-white that they wore in 1903, took part in four consecutive All-Irelands between 1926 and 1929, three of them against Kerry. The two also contested the first National

The Kildare team, All-Ireland champions in 1927.

League finals held at Croke Park in 1928 and 1929. While Kerry did the double in the League encounters Kildare won All-Irelands in 1927 and 1928. On the second occasion they became the first team to lift the newly-presented Sam Maguire cup. Kerry then reasserted their rising claim to be the most successful football county when they won four consecutive All-Irelands between 1929 and 1932. In the 1930s Cavan became the first power to emerge from Ulster when they won the 1933 and 1935 finals.

With the great teams came the great players including Jim Smith of Cavan, Bill Gannon and Jack Higgins of Kildare and Kerry's Joe Barrett, John Joe Sheehy and 'Danno' O'Keeffe. In hurling great rivalries were begun – Cork and Kilkenny, Cork and Tipperary, Kilkenny and Limerick – and some of the great legends of the game delighted the spectators – Lory Meagher of Kilkenny, Timmy Ryan and Mick Mackey of Limerick and Eudie Coughlan of Cork. In fact it was the first era of the star player. When in the late twentieth century Teams of the Millennium were being compiled for the GAA there were no players chosen from before the 1920s. One, Lory Meagher, began his playing career in the 1920s while eight emerged in the 1930s.

In the 1910–1920 period the big games at Croke Park drew crowds of between 12,000 and 20,000. With the increasing popularity of the games and with Croke Park as the most important venue in Ireland attendances grew. The hurling finals were attracting ever-increasing crowds. In 1931

The great Lory Meagher, then a selector, has a chat with Kilkenny goalie, Jimmy Walsh, during the 1945 Leinster Hurling Final.

Niall Quinn

FORMER DUBLIN MINOR HURLER AND IRISH SOCCER INTERNATIONAL

My father was a hurling man who played many a time in Croke Park where he won two minor All-Irelands and a National League with Tipperary. When I was young he brought me to all sorts of games there – football and hurling from club to Railway Cup. I played football there against Galway as a member of the Dublin Under-12 schools but I was only nine years of age. I scored 1-4 and the game ended in a draw. I played against Cork the following year and it was a draw again. I only scored a point that day and the boy marking me was Denis Irwin who played soccer for Ireland with me years later. I played in Croke Park too for my school team, St Peter's of Greenhills, and we won the Geraldine Cup there. Ciaran Walsh, who won an All-Ireland with Dublin in 1995, was our fullback. When I got a bit older I played in Croker with Drimnagh Castle School and we won a Dublin Title. Later on I was sent off in a Leinster Colleges game!

I always got in to Hill 16 free because the stilesman Ralph Seery knew me from playing football with Robert Emmets. The first All-Ireland I saw was the 1972 hurling final between Cork and Kilkenny but football took over with me for a while then because the Dublin team started winning and I went to see them every time.

I got on the Dublin minor hurling team of 1983 and we reached the All-Ireland final. We had great hopes against Galway but once our star Dessie Foley went off with an injured ankle we never played to our best and a good Galway team won the county's first title in the grade. It was the last hurling game I ever played.

The Hill was by far my favourite place and I had a corner of my own where I always went to watch matches. It was the first place I brought my children when the family came home from England – it always had a grip on me. We watched the 2003 Ladies football final from the same corner. A trip to Croke Park was almost a must every time I came home when I was playing soccer in England. I even brought Tony Cascarino and Andy Townsend there when they joined the Irish panel – it helped to make real Irish men out of them.

The place gave me a happy send-off before I headed to England the first day – it was 1983 and I was on the Hill on a very wet day watching the twelve Apostles from Dublin beat Galway in the All-Ireland football final.

Cork and Kilkenny fought the All-Ireland over three epic matches (the first and only time this happened) with a total of more than 90,000 attending the three matches. Dublin was taken over by the occasions:

> Nobody could walk through O'Connell Street and escape the infection of excitement over the heroic contest to be that thrilled the air. Thousands, literally thousands, of men were passing towards the Pro-Cathedral to mass on arrival from all parts of the country … When they came out they rushed the restaurants and tea shops; they poured into a cake shop and bought up all the buns and sandwiches. They swarmed on board trams, on the jaunting cars into taxi-cabs and private cars decorated with flags; they linked arms on the crowded pavements wearing ribbons and rosettes and golliwogs and little naked celluloid dolls whose hair grew the colours of Cork or Kilkenny – all swept northwards to Croke Park. It is impossible to stay behind; and one had to be carried along with it.[18]

The huge interest in the 1931 final had a knock-on effect in the following years. The 1932 final between Kilkenny and Clare attracted over 34,000 to the capital, while a new record for attendance at a hurling match was set in 1933 when 45,000 saw Kilkenny beat Limerick. The crowds

Action from the 1931 All-Ireland hurling final betweem Cork and Kilkenny.

Joe Lynch

FORMER MUSICAL DIRECTOR OF THE ARTANE BAND

I started off as a member of the Artane Boys Band in 1956 and only finished my association with the band in 1995 when I retired as Musical Director. The first time I played in Croke Park was in 1958 and I was a band member until 1962. There were incredible days with the great Offaly, Down and Armagh teams. The buzz, the excitement and the hairs standing up on the back of your neck would begin a week before the big days when rehearsals started.

The highlight of All-Ireland day was leading the teams on the parade around the field. Every section would be on their feet cheering for their team and sometimes you wouldn't even hear the music that you were playing, even though in those days the bands were bigger and we could have sixty or seventy in the band. I was drum major for the band for the last three years of my stint with the band and you would be in an awful fear that you would turn the wrong way or you would drop the mace or something would go wrong. Once somebody ran on the pitch. I had my mace in my right hand and he put a county flag in my other hand. I thought 'Oh my God, this will be showing favourtism', and I laid the flag down very gently.

In those days we loaded up a two-ton truck with school benches on a Saturday and brought them in and lay them along the sideline. That was our seating accommodation for the All-Ireland football or hurling final. We brought in our own benches and then went in on Monday and brought them back to the school. We started generally at twelve o'clock and didn't finish until five. And during that period of time we might have performed maybe for the best part of two hours.

For many years we could perform nothing other than Irish music. I can recall on one occasion with about seven or eight minutes to go before the parade going over to the Cusack Stand. I went through the ranks of the band and told them we would play Glenn Miller's 'In the Mood'. The crowd was unseated at the time and they swayed from left to right and we got a thunderous applause. When we finished, the Chief Steward at the time came and stood beside me and sort of looked way in the distance and said, 'Don't ever repeat anything like that in here again'.

Although we played in many other places each year I would say that the Artane Boys Band was definitely married to the GAA. I think it was a great combination. We gave what was expected of us hopefully all the time. We were very punctual, we went out to entertain, sadly we weren't allowed do what we wanted to do or what we thought the audience wanted but nevertheless whoever pays the piper calls the tune and you have to remember that.

One thing I remember was one night before an All-Ireland reading that Eamon de Valera was celebrating his ninetieth birthday. I stayed up until about three in the morning and I wrote the full instrumentation of Happy Birthday for every boy in the band. I remember going into Croke Park with great excitement and a huge spring in my step. I told them at Croke Park it was the President's birthday and could somebody make an announcement before the anthem and we will play Happy Birthday. I was told 'Definitely not! Definitely not!' So we went on and we did the minor game, we did the interval between both games and we did the parade of the teams. Just when we were ready to strike up the national anthem somebody announced over the PA system that we were celebrating the President's ninetieth birthday today. We stood on the pitch with no music, like eejits.

Another memory was the Armagh crowd singing 'The Boys from the County Armagh' at the 1977 football final. It was fantastic, especially at the Canal End – the colour, the flags, the bunting and how they sang it with gusto. It got to a stage that while I was conducting the band. I couldn't hear the band. I might as well have conducted the audience – the largest choir ever. On the opposite side was the time we were instructed to play 'Fainne Gael an Lae' for Kerry. No one knew the song (we were not allowed to play 'Rose of Tralee' or any other song in English). We played to a silent crowd. For weeks after people kept asking me 'What the hell did you play for Kerry?'

I still go back to Croke Park often. Players get a maximum of ten, twelve, fourteen years and then they are out of it. I had forty glorious years as man and boy and it is not easy to walk away from it.

attending the football finals were even larger. The replay of the 1926 Kerry-Kildare final was watched by 37,500 – 'brilliant weather, wild enthusiasm; gay throngs. Capital besieged with happy throngs sporting rival colours. Perfect order, glorious football …'[19] (For comparison it is interesting to note that during this period rugby internationals at Lansdowne Road were attracting crowds of 35,000.) When the same two counties met again in 1929 a then record crowd of 43,000 stretched the limits of the stadium. When the two met again in 1931 over 42,000 packed into Croke Park. In 1933 Cavan, with a large Ulster following, beat Galway in front of over 45,000.

THE CUSACK STAND

As the numbers of people attending the games increased so too did the money generated at the turnstiles. In the three football and five hurling matches just outlined over £23,000 were taken in gate receipts. Since the GAA had purchased the ground from Frank Dineen in 1913 it had spent over £30,000 on its prime asset at Jones' Road. However, it was inevitable that with increased income and attendances thoughts would turn to increasing accommodation at Croke Park (on safety grounds alone concern had been expressed about the ability of the stadium to cope with the crowds).

When the GAA celebrated its golden jubilee in 1934 the achievements of fifty years were looked back on with no small amount of understandable pride. That two of the main daily newspapers brought out substantial supplements in honour of the GAA was just one measure of the important position that the association had achieved in Irish society. In this jubilee year the faith in the future of the games was reasserted when it was decided in October that the eastern side of Croke Park would be redeveloped. Central Council asked Nicholas O'Dwyer, President of the Royal Institute of Civil Engineers in Ireland, to prepare and submit a scheme for an immediate extension of accommodation by 20,000 of which 5,000 should be seated. This led to the construction of a double-deck stand to be called the Cusack Stand after the founder of the GAA. Other changes included the provision of concrete terracing on Hill 16, a concrete wall enclosing the pitch and some new boundary walls and entrances. In order to build

Part of the procession celebrating the GAA Golden Jubilee at Croke Park in 1934.

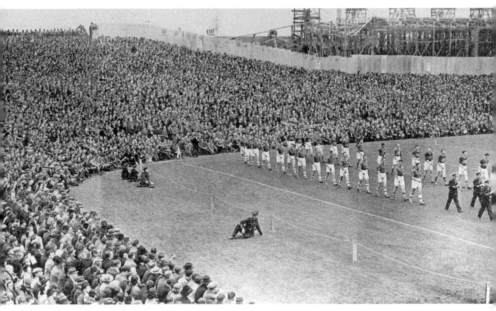

Cavan and Kerry parade before the 1937 All-Ireland final. Note the partly constructed Cusack Stand in the background.

the Cusack Stand it was necessary for the GAA to enter negotiations with Belvedere College to secure a strip of land 60 feet wide that had been sold to the College by Frank Dineen in order to finance the development of Jones' Road before its purchase by the GAA. In exchange for the strip of land a plot along the northern boundary of Croke Park was given to the school. By a later agreement another 20-foot strip was Acquired from Belvedere to provide access to the Cusack Stand from St James' Avenue. It was not to be the last time that the GAA had to recoup land Dineen had been forced to sell.

It was intended that the new stand would open in 1937 but a building worker's strike from April–October 1937 badly affected the construction timetable. Because of the strike the 1937 hurling final had to be held in Fitzgerald Park, Killarney. Over 43,000 watched Tipperary comprehensively defeat Kilkenny 3-11 to 0-3. Getting such large numbers to the location was not without its difficulties and there were long delays at Killarney train station. However, that the event was successfully accomplished was a testimony to the ability of the organisers. Concerned that the larger crowds attending football finals would cause many more difficulties GAA Secretary

Croke Park on the day of the official opening of the original Cusack Stand (left).

Pádraig O'Keeffe successfully negotiated with the Building Trades Council that labour be allowed to clear the site. Kerry played Cavan at Croke Park. The first game ended in a draw and Kerry won the replay. Over 100,000 people watched the two games.

On 21 August 1938 the Cusack Stand was officially opened. The opening day was an All-Ireland semi-final and appropriately teams from all four provinces took part in the senior and minor matches. It was a red-letter day for the GAA. All past All-Ireland winners were invited to the blessing ceremony. The GAA could boast that the Cusack Stand was the first *covered* double-decker stand in the country (in the 1920s the IRFU erected the first double-decker stand at Lansdowne Road but it was uncovered). The Cusack Stand, constructed of reinforced concrete, was 407 feet long, 52 feet wide and 79 feet high. The upper deck had seating for 5,000 while the lower deck was for standing only. In total 6,000 tons of concrete and 320 tons of reinforced steel were used in the stand with 115 tons of steel in the roof. Two sets of dressing rooms were constructed, each with showers, washbasins and a large plunge bath with hot water produced by electric heaters. A concrete wall 4 feet 6 inches tall surrounded the playing pitch. The slopes around the field were laid with concrete terracing and steel crush barriers were erected. The whole project had cost £52,000.

The original idea for a Cusack memorial of some sort was proposed by Waterford-man Dan Fraher at a GAA Annual Congress in late 1920s. Initially it was thought that a bust of the founder would be commissioned but when it was decided that a new stand was to be constructed at headquarters it seemed obvious it should be a fitting memorial to Cusack.

On its opening day the match programme paid tribute to Cusack and declared the stand was 'now open to all for appraisal. In its dedication it links the pioneers of the movement and in its magnitude it forecasts the unwavering devotion of native manhood to the historic games and Gaelic ideals of the nation'. The Cusack Stand, it declared, was 'the answer to the futile onslaught of Bloody Sunday commemorated by the Hogan stand'. It proclaimed 'the triumph of Gaelic faith and courage and determination to maintain the integrity and identity of the Irish nation' and reflected 'the confidence and courage of those presently in control of the fortunes of our distinctive pastimes and it will perpetuate the spirit which begot the Association over 50 years ago'.[20]

Croke Park was now almost completely surrounded by memories of its own past as well as by symbols of its association with Irish nationalism. GAA President Padraig McNamee addressed the gathering on the day of the opening of the stand;

We have already commemorated Archbishop Croke, our first patron, in the name of the Park itself. The Hogan Stand commemorates one who gave his life for the games and the cause of the Gael. Hill 16 is an ever-constant reminder to us of the gallant band who made the supreme sacrifice in order that this island of ours might be Gaelic and free. Today, in the naming of this stand, we pay deserved tribute to him whose prophetic vision and clear outlook we owe the birth of the Association to which we are all proud to belong.[21]

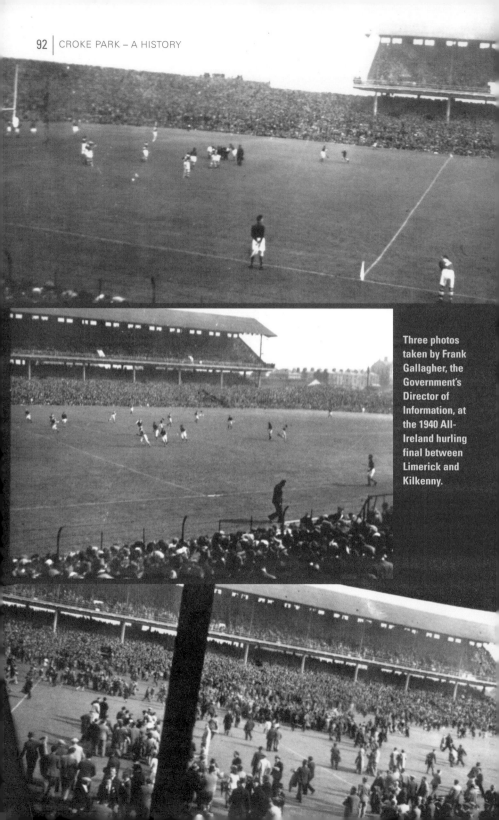

Three photos taken by Frank Gallagher, the Government's Director of Information, at the 1940 All-Ireland hurling final between Limerick and Kilkenny.

A 1941 artist's impression of the future of Croke Park.

The game played that day was between Kerry and Galway. It is notable for being the first broadcast from Croke Park by Micheál O'Hehir. O'Hehir's voice was to be inextricably linked with Gaelic games for four decades.

THE WAR YEARS

The years immediately after the construction of the Cusack Stand saw some of the greatest occasions at Croke Park. On 3 September 1939 Cork faced Kilkenny in what had now become a traditional rivalry in the All-Ireland final. Two days previously Hitler's Germany had invaded Poland. On the day of the match Britain declared war on Germany. At Croke Park Kilkenny led Cork into the second half when, in a portent of the Second World War, the last twenty minutes were played in a violent thunderstorm. In the final minute they were level but Kilkenny, in appalling conditions, scored two points to win what became known as the 'Thunder and Lightning' final.

Between 1941 and 1944 Cork achieved their unique hurling four-in-a-row. This legendary team included two of the greatest names to have graced the field at Croke Park – Christy Ring, who won eight All-Irelands in a career that spanned twenty-four years and Jack Lynch, the only man to win six consecutive All-Ireland medals (five for hurling and one for

D.J. Carey

KILKENNY HURLER

The first game I played in Croke Park was a football one for the Kilkenny schools under-twelve team in 1982. It was arranged that the schools would play Dublin in both football and hurling and I was delighted when I heard the matches would be in Croke Park. I had the choice between the two games but I had no difficulty in selecting football. The great Kerry team was a favourite of mine when I was growing up and I wanted to be like them. Tommy O'Brien took me to see them several times and I thought they were fantastic. To me they had style and seemed to enjoy playing football – they were all impressive and I liked the style of Mikey Sheehy, Sean Walsh and Jack O'Shea in particular. I scored two goals in that football match into the Hill 16 goal.

I thought that it was a thrill to tog out in the dressing room where all the stars in hurling and football had been – it was the one down in the corner under the old Hogan Stand. I had been there before to see hurling games – mostly Leinster finals when John Knox and Dick O'Neill organised a bus to bring all Gowran young lads along. I always had an ambition to play there again but it did not happen until 1988 when I was on the county minor hurling team when we beat Offaly in the Leinster final.

I am lucky that I have played there often since then. The place never gets dull and I think the whole ambience is the attraction – the stands, the dressing rooms and the crowds with your own in there among them. The pitch itself was the one to win on after a while. When I was young I had an ambition to play in Nowlan Park and later then it was nice to go further afield because I heard the stars talking about it. I remember Noel Skehan coming to present medals to us when we won the under twelve and he gave us great encouragement. It was great to listen and talk to somebody who had played and won in Croke Park. I think the Canal goal is the scoring one but I think of the whole place and the good times I had there with all the good players.

The strangest incident that happened to me at Croke Park was when I was asked to autograph a hurley outside the ground one day – that was not unusual but when I was signing it turned out to be my favourite stick that I had used that day. I don't know how the young lad got it but I did not give it back – the championship was not yet over.

My best memory of Croke Park has to be the opening ceremony of the Special Olympics – the atmosphere was wonderful and I could feel the pride of the athletes from all over the world. It was a great honour for me to lead another team on to my favourite pitch.

football). The first of their wins was in the 'Foot and Mouth' final of 1941. As a result of the travel restrictions imposed to stop the spread of the disease Cork were nominated to represent Munster. Dublin, nominated to represent Leinster, beat Galway to reach the final. However, they were no match for Cork who ran out easy winners 5-11 to 0-6. Cork defeated Dublin again in 1942. In the 1943 final they faced Antrim. As a gesture of solidarity during war-time rationing, team captains Mick Kennefick and Jimmy Walsh exchanged gifts of tea and bread and butter before the start of the match. The generosity did not last and Cork stormed home 5-16 to 0-4. The four-in-a-row was secured the following year when Cork again defeated Dublin at Croke Park.

In football it was the emergence of Roscommon that is most remembered of the war years. In 1943 they faced Cavan in front of 68,000 at Croke Park. In the *Irish Press* report it stated that in the build up referee Sergeant McKenna walked out and put the football 'dead centre' and walked away again. It continued, 'The sun glints on the brasses of the Artane Band. With a wild skirling the St Laurence O'Toole Piper's Band marches around while the white ball waits. A wild yell welcomed Cavan, and another one greets Roscommon …'[22] Roscommon captain Jimmy Murray later recalled his thoughts and feelings in the minutes before the start of the game:

> When I led Roscommon out it was a dream come true for me, and the whole thing struck me as awesome. The grass so green as I ran on to the field, and I felt so much alone that I glanced back to see if the rest of the lads were there at all. I'll never forget the crescendo of cheering; and most of the crowd had never seen the Roscommon colours till then. Then the march around, and the thoughts started to swim in my head. One moment I'd love to be up in the stand looking on. A terrible weight lay on your shoulders. You're carrying the honour for your family, your village, your county. I remember passing by Micheál O'Hehir's box and thinking of my native village, Knockcroghery, and thinking to myself, 'What are they doing at home just now?' I could imagine the neighbours around the old radio in the kitchen. My mother would be upstairs praying we'd win. My father would be down with the neighbours hoping.[23]

Above: The Volunteer Pipe Band prior to the 1943 All-Ireland hurling final.

Below: Eamon de Valera (third from left in second row) among the crowd attending the 1943 All-Ireland hurling final between Cork and Antrim. GAA President Seamus Gardiner is first on right in second row.

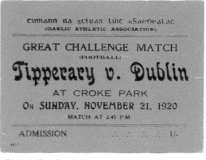

Bloody Sunday ticket.

A match ticket for a schools' final in 1933, illustrating that Croke Park was not just used for inter-county matches.

The programme cover from the 1913 All-Ireland final between Kerry and Wexford. This was the first final to be played at the re-named 'Croke Memorial Park'.

Poster for the 1923 Croke Park Fête.

Programme cover for the 1924 Rodeo.

Athletics programme covers from 1929 to 1931

The programme cover from the 1937
All-Ireland final replay played during
the construction of the Cusack Stand.

The programme cover from the 1944
All-Ireland football final between
Kerry and Roscommon.

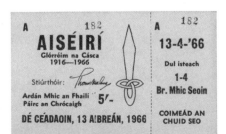

A ticket for the 1916 Rising fiftieth anniversary
commemoration in Croke Park in April 1966.

A ticket for the 1959 All-Ireland football final.

A poster advertising the 1943 football final.

The programme cover from the 1947 All-Ireland hurling final which proved to be one of the greatest ever although it was overshadowed by the Polo Grounds football final.

The programme cover from the 1957 All-Ireland hurling final between Kilkenny and Waterford.

The programme cover from the 1957 All-Ireland football final between Cork and Louth, the last final to be played in front of the original Hogan Stand.

The programme cover from the 1961 All-Ireland football final.

The cover of *Blát* magazine, published to commemorate the opening of the new Hogan Stand and the seventy-fifth anniversary of the GAA.

Right Croke Park ticket 1953.

Below: Croke Park ticket 1961.

D 199   D 199   D 199

17 - 3 - '53

Árdán Ciosóg

17-3-'53

Lá 'le Pádraig, 1953

This Portion Admits at

STILE

ST. JOSEPH'S AVE.

Árdán Ciosóg (res.) 5/-

This Portion Admits to **STAND**

RETAIN This Portion

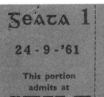

Seáta 1

24 - 9 - '61   24 - 9 - '61

This portion admits at

STILE

1, 2, 3 or 4

Taob-Líne 6/-
(Side-line)

RETAIN THIS PORTION

Cuireaò ʒo

Páirc an Crócaiʒ

Pádraʒ ó Caoimh
Árd-Rúnaí

Roinn — Suíoċán | Roinn — Suíoċán

Ardán Ciosóʒ

This portion
admits at
STILES
off
St. James's Ave.

mionúir 1.45 — Sinnsir 3.15

ALL-IRELAND FOOTBALL FINALS
24 - 9 - '61

24 - 9 - '61

Luaċ — 7/6

Pádraʒ ó Caoimh
Árd-Rúnaí

A selection of
Croke Park tickets:
1961 (left), 1963
(above) and 1970
(below).

Roinn — Suíoċán

Ardán Ciosóʒ
(UPPER DECK)

**ALL-IRELAND
FOOTBALL FINALS**
27 - 9 - '70

This portion
admits at
**SPECIAL
ENTRANCE**
from
St. James's Ave.

27 - 9 - '70

mionúir 1.30 — Sinsir 3.15

Luaċ — 20/-

Seán ó hÓcháin
Árd Rúnaí

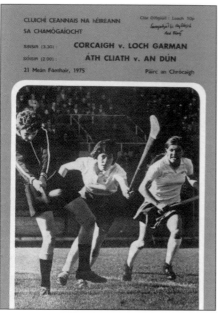

The programme cover from the 1975 All-Ireland camogie final.

The programme cover from the 1965 All-Ireland hurling final.

The programme cover from the 1977 All-Ireland football final between Dublin and Armagh.

The programme cover from the 1983 All-Ireland football final between Dublin and Galway.

Even as Croke Park is rebuilt, it plays host to historic scenes. In 1995 Clare win their first All-Ireland hurling title since 1914.

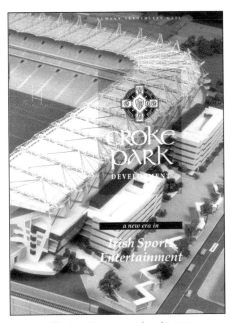

The brochure promoting the new Croke Park.

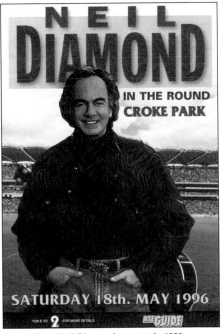

Poster for a Neil Diamond concert in 1996.

Above: The programme cover for American football from 1997.

Left: International Rules ticket from 1998.

Kilkenny and Offaly supporters in the newly-opened lower deck of the new Cusack Stand in 1998.

Left: The matches continue at Croke Park. A crowd scene from the 1997 All-Ireland football final between Kerry and Mayo.

Below: The GAA Museum which opened in 1998 as part of the development of the new Cusack Stand.

VIPs do a Mexican wave at the 1998 International Rules Series in Croke Park.

Tipperary and Kilkenny parade before the 1999 camogie final.

3 February 2007, Dublin and Tyrone parade out before the first match played under floodlights at Croke Park.

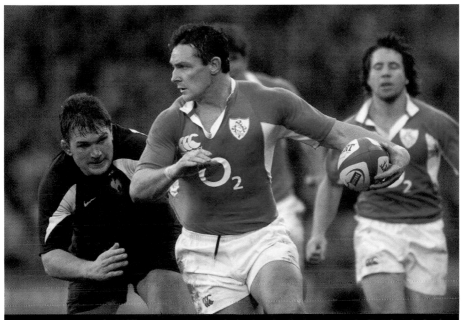

11 February 2007: History is made as rugby is played at Croke Park for the first time. Ireland lost narrowly to France.

24 February 2007: 'God Save the Queen' being played before the Ireland versus England rugby match at Croke Park.

The beginning of a new era, the 2002 All-Ireland hurling final between Clare and Kilkenny.

28 March 2007: Ireland's Richard Dunne celebrates Kevin Doyle's goal against Slovakia.

On 31 January 2009 a memorable evening at Croke Park started the festivities celebrating the 125th anniversary of the Gaelic Athletic Association.

Her Majesty Queen Elizabeth II, President Mary McAleese and Christy Cooney, President of the GAA, walk from the tunnel into Croke Park to view the ground on 18 May 2011, the second day of the State Visit to Ireland.

Her Majesty Queen Elizabeth II pictured with President Mary McAleese and Christy Cooney, President of the GAA, leaving Croke Park on 18 May 2011.

Croke Park is not just about the big names and the big days. Here girls of Scoil Lorcáin, Dublin, celebrate winning the 2012 Sciath Austin Finn. Each year some 1,200 players take part in the Cumann na mBunscol finals at GAA head quarters.

Kilkenny hurler Henry Shefflin, holder of nine All-Ireland medals from the field of play, holds aloft the 2012 Olympic Torch on 6 June 2012 on the Etihad Skyline at Croke Park.

Front row, from left, GAA President Seamus Gardiner, Dr Walsh Archbishop of Tuam, Pádraig O'Keeffe and Dan O'Rourke on the pitch before the 1943 football final between Cavan and Roscommon.

According to the newspaper article then, 'Sergeant McKenna picks up the ball. The bands fall back. The players run to their positions. Mr Seamus Gardiner, President, GAA, throws in the ball and then runs for it. Like one blast pent-up lungs are released. Blood calls to blood and Boyle consumes Ballyjamesduff.'[24]

The match, marred by missed chances, ended in a draw with Cavan's J. J. O'Reilly scoring a point with a last-minute free. With no set rule as to what should happen the referee, in front of a perplexed crowd, brought the two teams to the centre of the pitch and asked them if they would play extra time. Neither side wanted to continue and a replay was ordered. However, with no way of informing the crowd there was much confusion in the stands and on the terraces[25] (this scene led to the introduction of the first loudspeaker system at Croke Park for the replay[26]).

The replay was played in front of a smaller crowd and Roscommon, led by Phelim Murray, Donal Keenan (later President of the GAA) and Frankie Kinlough beat Cavan 2-6 to 2-2. While on a mountainside in Italy Billy Doonan listened on his military radio, in Portlaoise Prison there was an unusual listening audience:

MY MEMORIES

Ryan Tubridy

RTÉ BROADCASTER

My father was born in Galway but we were not a big GAA family except on weekends when Galway were playing in Croke Park. I remember going with my father and buying flags and loads of chocolate before going into the match. We were often on Hill 16 and when I was young I had the best view of all – sitting on my father's shoulders and, of course, eating the chocolate.

The enormity of the place always impressed me with swathes of people everywhere I looked. Sometimes I spent more time studying the people than watching the match. I thought the intensity that was obvious on the faces of spectators was fascinating to watch as the fortunes of the game changed at pace. I remember the four great games between Dublin and Meath in the 1991 Leinster Championship and the custard cream biscuits that I ate while the players were putting on the wonder shows.

I studied Roman History and sometimes the idea flashed into my mind that Croke Park was the latter-day coliseum. It seemed to me at times that it was a venue for gladiatorial struggles and I loved it for that.

There was something special about the roar of the crowd. I found the referees interesting as a study topic also and in my mind I elevated them to the status of emperor. The way they were able to make life and death decisions swung me to that way of thinking. And it was always in the back of my mind that my cousin Mick Tubridy won an All-Ireland medal in Croke Park with the Cork footballers in 1945. He played in the half-forward line and Jack Lynch was a member of the same team. Mick was a Clare man and must have been a great sportsman because he was equally good as a showjumper.

Here were men doing sentences from six months to twenty years and life, all convicted of some crime, and still how human they were. No schoolboy at Croke Park had more enthusiasm. When Roscommon scored, how the convicts of the West cheered. When Cavan equalised, the guilty of the North-East raised the roof. Although betting was strictly prohibited, somehow the supporters of Roscommon had double rations that evening, while the Cavan fans mourned in hunger.[27]

Andrew Holden (centre), his father Andrew (left) and Rich Reynolds at the All-Ireland semi-final between Wexford and Cavan in 1945. Young Andrew went on to play international hockey for England.

In 1944 Roscommon faced Kerry in an eagerly anticipated contest. Despite the war-time restrictions on travel 79,245 people were crammed into Croke Park. The night before Dublin was packed with people 'up for the match'. With all accommodation taken hundreds slept in doorways around O'Connell Street as others took refuge in Garda stations or made their way to the suburbs to ask homeowners to put them up. Churches were packed, hotels and restaurants took a rich harvest while sellers of team favours and ballads 'raked it in':

> It was rural Ireland's invasion of the Metropolis but Dublin people, too, flocked to Croke Park in larger numbers than ever before. Turnstiles were clogged by the weight of human traffic and by three o'clock many entrances had to be closed. Looking at that packed ground from my seat on the Cusack Stand I let my mind go back in fancy to twenty years before when I saw Kerry and Dublin clash for the 1923 title and thought of the crowds of those days. They were big for the times and the enthusiasm was grand after years of fighting, but 1944 put it all in the shade. Double the crowd and the enthusiasm far more infectious, for the West had sent its hostings to cheer on the Connaught men in their bid to return the title for the second year. The Southerners, too, were there in their thousands, with Ulster strong in its support of the national games and Leinster always to the fore well represented. The while my memory was travelling back to other great hostings, Roscommon and Kerry were parading before the biggest crowd ever to attend a sporting fixture in this country.[28]

At Croke Park the gates were closed twenty minutes before the start of the match and the thousands locked out had to make do with listening to Micheál O'Hehir's commentary. He set the scene:

The crowd surpasses all hopes. They have been pouring into Croke Park since noon. I have just learned that the gates have been closed, and here is something new – we are broadcasting not only to you at your wireless set, but also to the thousands outside the gates, unable to gain admission.

The crowd on Hill 16 is jammed tightly; the Cusack Stand is full and, of course, the Hogan Stand has its usual quota of personalities of the political, sporting and general spheres of life. The Long Stand is full, and one crowded-out enthusiast is climbing up a steel support and will soon be sitting on a girder. Up, up he goes and as he reaches his object the crowd give him a loud cheer.[29]

Also in attendance were Dr E. Hempel, the representative of the German government in Ireland, and John Maffey, the UK government representative. They were treated to one of the most exciting finals ever. The scores were level on three different occasions during the game but Roscommon won their second All-Ireland 1-9 to 2-4. Roscommon were back in Croke Park for the 1946 All-Ireland when they again faced Kerry. Once again it went to a replay with Kerry emerging victors.

Over 335,000 people had watched three All-Irelands and two replays involving Roscommon. During the Emergency nearly 600,000 people attended the finals in Croke Park and paid over £48,000. At a time when few trains ran and cars were off the road the attendances achieved were remarkable – epic journeys made on foot, horseback, bicycle, turf lorry and cattle cart. The new Cusack Stand had played its own role in this era by helping to accommodate record crowds for the football finals of 1938 and 1944 as well as near record ones for the hurling finals. As a result the debt incurred in the construction of that stand was paid off in its entirety by 1945. In 1946 the Central Council of the GAA recorded a surplus of £12,000. Thoughts were already turning to further extending the accommodation at headquarters.

CHAPTER FOUR

1947–1982

Kerry fans at Croke Park in the 1950s.

POLO GROUNDS FINAL

The 1947 All-Ireland hurling final between Cork and Kilkenny is regarded as one of the greatest to have been played. One Monday newspaper headline called it the 'Never-to-be-Forgotten Game'.[1] The Cork side, including Christy Ring, Jack Lynch, Sean Condon and Tom Mulcahy, were at the tail end of one of their county's greatest eras having won five out of the previous six All-Irelands while Kilkenny, who had lost their three previous finals, featured among others Jim Langton, Terry Leahy, Mark Marnell, Jim Donegan and Paddy Lennon. The match was slow to get going. At half-time Kilkenny led 0-7 to 0-5. The second half saw the sporting tide ebb and flow. Coming to the end of normal time Cork led by a point and seemed to have edged to victory. However, a late free from Kilkenny's Terry Leahy levelled the score. In 'lost time' Cork drove the ball up the field but Paddy Grace cleared to Leahy who, from 65 yards out, sent over the winning point. Seamus King, author of *A History of Hurling,* wrote that it 'produced hurling that will live forever in the memory of those who were privileged to see it'.[2]

However, when 1947 is mentioned in GAA circles it is not the hurling final which generally springs to mind but the football final played thousands of miles away from Croke Park. On 4 September 1947 the Cavan and Kerry football teams boarded the Cunard-White ship *Mauretania* for New York. On 14 September they played the first All-Ireland final to be played outside Ireland and the first to be played away from the Jones' Road venue since 1907 when Dublin beat Cork in Athy. The GAA's historic decision to transport what had become the largest sporting event in Ireland across the Atlantic was taken both to commemorate the centenary of the Famine and to help revitalise Gaelic games in America which had declined because of a falling off of Irish emigration to America during the Second World War. The Polo Grounds final was one of the great GAA achievements. Financially it brought in considerable income (the trip raised over $150,000[3]) but the symbolism and prestige of bringing what had become the main event of the GAA season to the glamorous shores of America was even more important.

The attendance at the Polo Grounds was less than hoped for with just 35,000 showing up. However, at home in Ireland hundreds of thousands tuned in at 8.30pm to listen to Micheál O'Hehir's live commentary broadcast from New York. To make up for the fact that people were not able to see the final, Gael Linn were employed to film it for showing in cinemas back home. This was the beginning of annual filming, and later televising, of GAA finals.

After missing a year, interest in the 1948 football final was phenomenal. Cavan, the victors of New York, faced the newly-emergent Mayo. Applications for tickets poured in to General Secretary Pádraig O'Keeffe's office at Croke Park. On the morning of the final a queue started to form at the ground at 9.00am. At 1.45 the gates were closed. Inside, the crowd were entertained by the Artanc Boys Band who played an eclectic mix of tunes that included the 'Davis Centenary March', selections from operas of Balfe, 'Sousa on Parade', excerpts from the 'Melodies of Victor Herbert', 'Roisin Dhu', 'Trial by Jury' and 'Croppy Boy'.[4]

Outside 25,000 were locked out of headquarters. With only limited reserved seating available most would have travelled on the day of the match hoping to pay at the turnstiles. Outside all they could do was rely on local residents to sympathetically open their windows so they could hear the action described by wireless amidst the partly muffled cheers and groans from inside the park. It may have been little consolation that the match failed to live up to the lofty expectations. Public interest is no guarantee of a great occasion and the match was described as 'hard, grim in places, and certainly exciting, it contained little first-class football. The high wind, close tackling, and incessant frees – 52 in the hour – robbed it of much of the spectacle'.[5] Cavan, featuring the great defender John Joe O'Reilly, midfielder Simon Deignan and Mick Higgins in the forward line faced Padraig Carney (who scored the first penalty in an All-Ireland final) and Mick Flanagan, Eamon Mongey and Tom Langan. Cavan, who had led by 3-2 to no score at half-time, only just stumbled to victory 4-5 to 4-4.

PÁDRAIG O'KEEFFE'S VISION FOR CROKE PARK

The year 1949 saw the beginning of an inevitable major redevelopment of Croke Park. As early as 1945 the GAA had decided that Croke Park needed to be enlarged to cope with the ever-increasing crowds. From a situation when for much of the 1920s and the first half of the 1930s crowds for the big games were between 25,000 and 50,000, the late 1930s

Pádraig O'Keeffe, General Secretary of the GAA from 1929–1964.

and 1940s saw attendances rise to between 50,000 and 80,000 for the football finals and 30,000 to 70,000 for the hurling finals. The games had never been more popular. This situation was reflected in the balance sheet of the amateur association. By the end of the 1940s the assets of Central Council totalled £167,000, with liabilities of just £4,500.[6] In such an environment the GAA was in an excellent financial situation from which to tackle the redevelopment of its most valuable physical asset.

The redevelopment of Croke Park was largely driven by the energy and vision of Pádraig O'Keeffe, the General Secretary of the GAA from 1929 to 1964. O'Keeffe was slim, quiet spoken, very religious and a teetotaller. Born in Roscommon, he spent much of his early life in Cork. A founder player-member of the famous Nemo Rangers club, he attended his first

All-Ireland in 1912 when Cork lost to Kilkenny. During the War of Independence he was sentenced to fifteen years' penal servitude in Parkhurst Prison for republican activities. On his release he threw himself into organising the GAA in Cork. O'Keeffe was appointed secretary of the GAA in 1929 on the death of Luke O'Toole and for more than three decades he was to exert huge influence over the GAA. Nowhere was this influence more in evidence than at Croke Park.

Croke Park held a special place for O'Keeffe. At all times he appreciated the important role it played in the Association. One contemporary commented, 'He lived in Croke Park. I felt he was often tempted to sleep there.'[7] Another wrote that Croke Park occupied 'a particularly warm corner of his heart. You could know how much he loved every stone and every blade of grass there by the way, in conversation, he was wont to refer to it, not as Croke Park, but simply and solely as "the Park".'[8] On match days he could pop up anywhere from a broken stile on Jones' Road to the centre of the pitch. He rarely occupied his reserved seat in the Hogan Stand. From a time when he had to 'slave and write and publicise in order to fill the Park', his biggest problem had become how to cope with the demand for tickets. The opening of the Cusack Stand in 1938 had only briefly met the demand. In the late 1940s it became his ambitious wish that Croke Park would be big enough to hold everyone who wanted to see an All-Ireland final. After his death in 1964 many believed that 'Croke Park is the obvious monument to the memory of Pádraig O'Keeffe'.[9] The realisation of this vision was a ground that was to remain virtually unchanged from 1959 to the recent modernisation of the stadium.

Work on the redevelopment began in September 1949 when O'Keeffe employed temporary staff to look after ticketing arrangements for the Meath-Cavan football final. With his desk cleared he concentrated on making the necessary arrangements for the first phase of what was, for the time, a revolutionary vision for Croke Park. On 27 October O'Keeffe announced to the press that a 'bigger Croke Park' was on the way.[10] According to one commentator at the end of the programme of expansion about 'the only thing left to do would be to have a fleet of glass helicopters hovering in the air above the pitch and all Ireland would be accommodated and nobody would have a grouse'.[11]

The redevelopment had to take into consideration some stark geographical facts. The ground at the back of the Hogan Stand side was private

Marcus de Búrca

AUTHOR OF *THE GAA: A HISTORY*

I was born in 1927 and attended my first All-Ireland hurling final in 1934. How do I know? Because the Dublin goalie was our daily bread-delivery man!

Even before he migrated to Dublin my father was a close friend of 'Paddy-O' [Paddy O'Keeffe], General Secretary 1929–1964. They had met in Cork when my father was in University College Cork, pre First World War.

In Croker of the 1930s I was allowed to run wild. I cannot claim to have been there in the days of the grazing sheep. But I do vividly recall Curran's horse, which pulled the mower of Boer War vintage. Inevitably came the great day when I got rid of Chicky Curran and Curran's son Jimmy and I went round and round the sacred grass until the poor nag tired and I was banished to the shop opposite on Jones' Road owned by two old women who were cajoled into giving us credit (Curran's, of course) and parting with bottles of lemonade and bars of Fry's Cream Chocolate! Is it any wonder I got diabetes in my fifties?

The old Hogan Stand was a very exclusive place to the day it was demolished. Paddy-O had a special seat, which (as his daughters will confirm) he rarely occupied, so I could move into the exclusive O'Keeffe area and chat up the aforesaid daughters.

I can remember three pillars of the Free State who had seats reserved for life. J.J. Keane, of Geraldines fame in the 1890s and the founder of the NACA in 1922, could pass as a well-fed double of Joe Stalin. He never talked to anyone bar O'Keeffe; just sat immobile with his rolled-up umbrella. The latter he used occasionally to trip wild youngsters who crossed his path of vision. Keane was known to his contemporaries as Hay and Straw; he operated from the loft of a business house in Smithfield where he sold (you guessed it) hay and straw to the cattle-dealers. In this 'lofty' arena the Olympic Council of Ireland (over which Keane presided) met frequently!

J.J. Walsh of Cork city also had 'his' seat. He was a flashy dresser, often sporting a Bing Crosby hat and with check suits that would dazzle you. He talked out loud on everything from athletics to Dev, much to the embarrassment of Paddy-O and J.J. Keane. He could roll his Rs far better that Pat Fanning, and became quite partisan – often standing up to lecture the ref 100 yards away – when Cork were playing!

Denis Guiney of Clery's Store was mercifully less voluble from his sacred seat. He would direct his venom at Paddy-O, and was intentionally cool to Walsh. Because of his girth, once he lowered himself into his seat, he never moved till the final whistle. 'Sonny, will you hold my stick?' were the only words he ever spoke to me as he extricated his enormous frame from a seat designed for someone half his size.

By far my favourite character in old Croker was Martin O'Neill, appointed Secretary to the Leinster Council the year I was born. In 1984, when I was compiling the Council's centenary record, I drove down to meet him in his Wexford home. A long-time widower, Martin cooked a three-course lunch I still remember. I reminded him of all the chocolate and ice-cream he gave me fifty years before! He told me how this began: one day (it must have been in the early 1930s) my mother pleaded with him to take me 'downstairs' as someone (I suspect J.J. Keane) complained his spinal chord was in danger from continuous kicking from an unidentified brat!

property. There was a railway behind one goal and a canal behind the other. On the remaining side were the Cusack Stand and Hill 16, and behind the Cusack Stand lay pitches owned by Belvedere College. Therefore, space was at a premium. The Croke Park development programme began with the construction of terracing at the Canal End. An English architectural firm, Jackson and Edmonds, based in Birmingham, was given the contract. Despite the international reputation of the firm, which had had experience in designing stadiums around the world, there were rumblings from some about the break with GAA ethos. The Secretary of the Engineers Association of Ireland expressed dismay on behalf of his members that an Irish firm was not awarded the contract.[12] When the new terrace opened in 1950, it increased the capacity of Croke Park by 14,000.

Two years later the small Nally Stand was opened. Located at the north-west corner of the ground it was named after Pat Nally. Nally was a leading figure in the Irish Republican Brotherhood and a founder member and secretary of the Land League. He was also a legendary athlete. It was as a result of a conversation he had with Michael Cusack in the Phoenix Park, bemoaning the decline in native athletics, that led to the founding of the Gaelic Athletic Association. In 1884, when he was twenty-six years old, he was convicted of taking part in the 'Crossmolina Conspiracy' – the attempted murder of a land agent – and was sentenced to penal servitude. Had he not been in prison he would certainly have played a very active role in the new Association. In April 1891, as a result of his treatment in jail, he died in Mountjoy Prison.

BEHIND THE SCENES

On the occasion of a major fixture, behind the scenes, the staff of Croke Park made the day work. Groundsman Jimmy 'Chicky' Curran (who remained as groundsman in Croke Park until 1967) got the pitch ready for each match, readied the goalnets, oiled the seventy turnstiles. Arrangements were made for the 250 stewards who would be on duty. On the day before an All-Ireland Final Willie Rock would be summoned to O'Keeffe's office. A well-known figure around Croke Park, Rock was the 'Voluntary Custodian of the Ball'. Since O'Keeffe had taken up his position, there had been a traditional ceremony when O'Keeffe would present him with four match balls for the next day. Before the start of the match Rock, in his familiar bowler hat (the subject of more than a few jeers and taunts), would stride to the centre of the field to present a match ball to the referee (keeping the other three on the sideline should one burst or not be returned from the crowd).[13] Willie's son John had been working the scoreboard for fifteen years by the early 1950s. In the 1980s the family connection with Croke Park was resumed when John's nephew, Barney Rock, played centre stage at Croke Park when he was on the Dublin team that won the 1983 All-Ireland final.

After the expectation of the build up to a big match day was over and the excitement had passed, Croke Park took on a completely different hue. The day after the 1953 football final, for example, the Kerry team made its victorious way home for the customary parades, receptions and

Willie Rock, 'voluntary custodian of the ball', at Croke Park.

speeches. Meanwhile the staff at Croke Park began the clean-up operation. How different the empty stadium looked and felt. An *Irish Press* reporter visiting Croke Park in the aftermath quoted from a Tom Moore poem: 'I feel like one who treads alone/ Some banquet hall deserted'. He described the scene, 'Jimmy Curran, the groundsman and his staff, were about to suspend their cleaning up operations at lunch hour and thousands of scavenging seagulls just sat there on the green sward waiting for the men to go. As soon as they did, they made an all-out assault on the deserted stands and enclosures … At intervals tons of papers, cigarette cartons, ice cream tubs, programmes, bottles, broken tea flasks and other sundries had been swept up in small heaps ready to be carried away on wheel barrows. Everywhere smoke was rising from little fires where old newspapers, programmes and chocolate boxes were being burned.' Brooches, gloves, belts, handkerchiefs and other personal belongings were collected and a notice put in the newspapers asking people to contact Croke Park if they had lost something.[14]

A CLASSIC ERA

In many ways the 1950s was a classic era for the GAA and it was in this decade that Croke Park became a symbol of Irish life. The ground at Jones' Road became almost a physical expression of Irish identity. It was quintessentially Irish, a national reference point and part of the definition of mainstream Ireland that was largely rural, conservative, nationalist and Catholic. The All-Ireland Final was where these values were reaffirmed in the twice-annual rite. The Croke Park timetable for its red-letter days reads almost like a religious liturgy:

12.00 Gates open.

12.05 Artane Band renders selections.

1.15 Minor teams take the field.

1.20 Massed pipers lead minor teams into position.

1.30 Minor game starts. At half-time Artane band perform.
At full-time of minor match massed pipers parade.

2.55 Arrival of President – Artane Band plays 'Presidential Salute'.

2.58 Bands march into position at Cusack Stand side.

3.03 Senior teams take the field.

3.08 Teams march around into position.

3.12 Archbishop of Cashel with President of the GAA enters field, band play 'Faith of our Fathers' followed by the National Anthem.

3.15 Archbishop starts the game.[15]

Other events held at Croke Park reaffirmed this image of the GAA. In 1929 it hosted the national celebrations of the centenary of Catholic Emancipation. In 1949 it hosted the Golden Jubilee Pioneer Total Abstinence Association of the Sacred Heart. Ten years later they held another rally when the ground was turned into 'a vast open-air church when the men and women, boys and girls, soldiers and nurses, Gardai and bandsmen, kneeling in brilliant sunshine, made a public act of thanksgiving to the Sacred Heart for the blessing bestowed through the Pioneer

Goal-mouth action during the 1950 All-Ireland
football final between Louth and Mayo

MY MEMORIES

Mairead McAtamney

FORMER ANTRIM CAMOGIE CAPTAIN AND WINNER OF
TWO ALL-IRELAND MEDALS

We were a Gaelic family in Antrim all involved in sport so there was talk about Croke Park in our house nearly all the time. My first memory is of arriving there in 1944 as a player at the age of sixteen when Dublin beat us in the final. I must say I was overawed at being there not to mind having the privilege of playing there. I remember how wonderful it was to step onto the pitch and even though the number of spectators was small the excitement was great.

We won the next three and again in 1956 but the best of all was the replay of the 1967 final with Dublin. It was played as a curtain raiser to the Oireachtas final and there was a very big attendance. I think it was the best game I ever played – it was one of those days that everything went right and I scored four or five points from midfield. I have been going there for years as a spectator and would never miss any of the big games in hurling or football as well as camogie. We talk about the wonderful place a lot and look forward to the visits.

The Artane Boys Band in the 1950s.

Above: Armagh supporters before the 1953 All-Ireland final.

Below: Kerry captain, James Murphy, kissing the Archbishop's ring in 1953.

Above: The 1954 All-Ireland football final between Meath and Kerry.

Below: Jack Mangan of Galway lifts the Sam Maguire trophy after the 1956 All-Ireland football final. Note the plaque to Michael Hogan in the centre of the crowd.

Above: The Croke Park staff in 1958: back row from left, Jimmy Curran and Seán O'Síacháin; front row from left, Bríd Ní Mhuircheartaigh, Pádraig O'Keeffe and Eileen McDonald.

Below: Another view of the Croke Park Staff in 1958, with the Hogan Stand in the background.

The Patrician Year mass in 1961.

Survivors of the 1916 Rising commemorating its fiftieth anniversary in Croke Park in 1966.

Movement's 60 years of activity'.[16] Two years later the Papal Legate celebrated the Mass for the Patrician Year at Croke Park. In May 1956 (during *An Tostal*), *The Pageant of Cuchulann*, written by Denis Johnston, played in the ground for five nights. In 1961 the *Pageant of St Patrick* was staged there.

Perhaps the most symbolically important occasion came in 1966 when Croke Park was used as the venue for *Aiseiri Gloir Reim na Casca* as part of the commemorations of the fiftieth anniversary of the 1916 Rising. The pageant was the creation of Abbey Theatre producer Tomás MacAnna and depicted Ireland's 'historical struggle' for independence from the United

More scenes from the Patrician Year Mass in 1961.

Irishmen of the 1798 Rising to the setting up of the first Dáil in 1919. Opened by President de Valera on 12 April it was a performance of epic proportions. A cast of 800 played out the scenes in front of a huge backcloth (150 feet wide and 50 feet high) of the General Post Office. The crowd appropriately sat in the Hogan Stand, itself a poignant reminder of the violence of the past. The narrator, 'the voice of history', was played by Micheál MacLiammor, while the leading actors of Ireland (including Ray MacAnally who played the part of Pearse) were supported by members of the Defence Forces.

According to one newspaper report, from the re-enactment of the 1798 Rising, 'the pungent smell of the dummy powder and the cracking of the

Frank Hughes

MATCH DAY STAFF

Well, I am over sixty years connected with the GAA. I've lived in the area all my life and I was born and reared on Clonliffe Road. Coming up and down along the road and going into Croke Park and having a look around, I got to know the ground staff there. Jimmy Curran and his father were the ground staff at the time. I first worked there sweeping the stands and doing general work around the place. I was twenty-six or twenty-seven I did not get full-time work. You'd get a couple of days and then you'd be knocked.

You would come in on a Monday after a match and Jimmy would be there and his father and Christy Lynch, and you'd line up and they'd say, 'You're on today', but maybe if you got too many days the last week you wouldn't get the same amount the following week. Sometimes you'd think you'd get the week out of it, but it wouldn't be so dirty and you might only get three days.

We never got free passes for matches, but before each All-Ireland Miss Moriarty would come down to you and ask, 'How many tickets do you want?' She'd say to come to her on a certain day at a ten o'clock. Now you had to be there at ten. Not five to. Not five past. Ten o'clock was the time.

As Croke Park got bigger and bigger I was brought in more and more. I came in looking after offices and working inside the stores doing different things around the place like getting boardrooms ready.

One job that I was given, and still have today, is to pump the footballs. I just do it with an ordinary pump. I don't use a pressure gauge but just check the pressure with my thumb. I do it before every match and I have never been questioned. I also put up the flags on match day. The only objection I ever had was with the Aussie flag. When I'd seen the Union Jack on it I said, 'No, I will not fly that flag'. I didn't want to fly it. And it took four or five days before I eventually got around to flying it anyway because I was told it was supposed to be only an emblem.

Oh, Croke Park is a great place for memories. When I started here the only people working here were Miss Moriarty, Paddy O'Keeffe and Seán O'Síocháin. It is a much bigger place now, but I am enjoying it today as I did then.

hundreds of rifles in battle aroused feelings of rebellion and joy. This was a feeling I believe everyone in the audience, even in the teeth of the bitter cold, felt here and held until Pearse's forced surrender.'[17] Another wrote that brilliant scene followed brilliant scene and that 'the seizure of the GPO in particular, and its subsequent sustained attack by the British amid storm and shot and shell, culminates in the great building engulfed in flames, is almost terrifying in its realism'.[18] At the end of the week a 'Children's Day' was held on which 15,000 boys and girls headed by the Artane Band and the band of the Irish Transport and General Workers Union marched from O'Connell Street to Croke Park to witness the spectacle. Later in the year the GAA paid its own special tribute to the men of 1916 when they invited all 600 survivors to the All-Ireland hurling final. The crowd of 68,000 joined the Artane Band in a moving rendition of '*Oro Se do Beatha Abhaile*'.

Non-GAA sporting occasions held in Croke Park were more ecumenical in nature. In November 1953 an American football game held in aid of the Irish Red Cross society was held at Croke Park. The teams were made up of American soldiers based in England. In 1973 a youth version of the *Tailteann* Games was held. Called the Willwood Games after its main sponsor, it ran from 24 June to 15 July. On 19 July 1972 a boxing programme was organised for Croke Park. Among those included on the

Runners competing in the Willwood Games in 1973.

bill was Joe Bugner, Charlie Jordan and John Conteh. The headline bout was between Muhammad Ali and Al Blue Lewis that was scheduled to go ten three-minute rounds. Ali was using the bout as preparation for a fight against Floyd Patterson in New York in August. The winner of that would face Joe Frazier in a world-title decider.

In the 1950s Croke Park witnessed some of the greatest GAA matches. While the 1940s is best remembered for its football matches, the 1950s was a decade when hurling captured the popular imagination and has provided some of the sport's most enduring memories to this day. The hurlers of Wexford provided many of these.

INTERNATIONAL
HEAVYWEIGHT CONTEST

MUHAMMAD ALI

AL BLUE LEWIS

CROKE PARK, DUBLIN
WEDNESDAY, 19th JULY, 1972

Souvenir
PROGRAMME

The programme cover from the Muhammad Ali fight in Croke Park in July 1972.

Widely regarded as one of the most glamorous teams to play the game their skill, sportsmanship and fervent followers drew the support of neutrals. The Wexford hurlers, featuring the three Rackard brothers, took on the might of the established counties and contested three consecutive All-Irelands between 1954 and 1956. In 1954 they faced Cork in front of 84,856. To this day it still remains a record attendance at a hurling match. Writer and journalist Benedict Kiely wrote in his match report that 'there weren't too many flags on the Hill. Too closely packed the people looked. If you raised your arm over there to hold a flag, you'd have to keep it up for the rest of the day like Moses on the mountain during the battle.'[19] Wexford lost the game by three points and Cork's Christy Ring became the first player to win eight All-Ireland hurling medals.

In 1955 Wexford faced Galway. While the match was close for much of the game Wexford pulled away in the closing stages winning 3-13 to 2-8. For the first time entertainment, including Irish-dancing, was provided at half-time during this match.[20] Rarely had a victory been greeted with such delight by the neutral follower of the games. Wexford had come close on a number of occasions to a breakthrough. At last they had achieved their day in the sun, something everyone could support. However, the Wexford team of this era is best remembered for the 1956 final. Once again they faced the traditional power of Cork in a match that has become one of the yardsticks against which subsequent games are measured. By all accounts it was one of the sport's classic encounters. The 'Yellow Bellies' of Wexford charged into a seven-point lead but at half-time Cork had narrowed the gap to just three. In the second half Cork drew level and then took the lead. The final minutes were taut with tension. The match's defining moment came when Wexford goalkeeper Art Foley made one of the greatest saves in Croke Park history from Christy Ring. Had Ring scored Cork would have taken the lead and possibly won the match. But Foley cleared the ball up-field, where Nicky Rackard scored the goal that sealed victory for Wexford. Ring ran to shake Foley's hand and in a great moment at the end of the match Bobbie Rackard and Nick O'Donnell carried Christy Ring, their great opponent, shoulder high off the pitch.

Of course, hurling did not have a monopoly on the great occasion. In 1955 the Kerry-Dublin football final set a new attendance record when officially 87,102 paid to see the match. However, like many other attendance figures of the time the unofficial figure was much higher. Two entrances that had been closed to stop people coming in were forced open and thousands rushed in – a fairly common occurrence at the time. In addition there was the usual uncounted number of children lifted over the turnstiles in the great Croke Park tradition that has only been recently stopped. Indeed so ingrained had the tradition become that today it is still necessary for the stadium authorities to erect signs instructing people that children have to have a ticket to gain admission to the stadium. Outside Ireland thousands of emigrants listened in to the match on WNYC radio in New York. Missionary priests were catered for by a broadcast of the match relayed on Radio Brazzaville in North Africa. As the closing lines of the National Anthem merged with the cheering crescendo of 'Up Kerry' and 'Come on Dublin', Dr Moynihan, Bishop of Kerry, threw in the ball to start the hour's football.[21] Kerry won the match but Dublin had only to wait three years when, with a team of native Dublin players, they won their first football championship since 1942.

With the crowds increasing in size the behaviour of the spectators came into focus. The people standing on the terraces or sitting in the stands are an essential ingredient to modern sport. Far from providing a passive

Bertie Ahern

FORMER TAOISEACH

The first time I remember being in Croke Park was 1959 when Dublin were the reigning All-Ireland champions. I'd say I was there before that but I can't recall. Everybody's guess would be that I was on the Hill but we were always Canal people. My father was a Corkman and had his own spot for years, four steps in front of the scoreboard at the Canal End and we went along with him. It was a normal part of the week to have your back to the weather and the canal and be looking at the match towards the Hill. I really enjoyed watching the 1963 All-Ireland final when Dublin beat Galway with a late goal from Gerry Davey.

The brothers and myself often went to the Hill for small matches, like club games on Friday nights, and it was great fun and value. Those games drew big crowds. The Hill became a favourite with me in later years and I stood there many a time when I was a TD and Minister. I remember the 1977 All-Ireland final with Armagh when you could say that the regulars were evicted from the Canal area. It was handed over to Armagh, but I must say that they brought great colour to the occasion with the bright saffron flags and banners. The Hill was really alive that day and the great Dublin team that had beaten Kerry in the semi-final and in the 1976 final got the reception of a lifetime.

When I was confined to the Ard Comhairle section of the magnificent Hogan Stand, I often cast an envious glance at the Hill on days when Dublin were playing.

backdrop crowds have the capacity to lift a team and elevate a spectacle. They also had the capacity to turn nasty, to taunt, to jeer. On a number of occasions they were urged by the GAA to act only on their most positive instincts while at Croke Park. As early as 1931 the GAA put notices in the papers requesting that their patrons act with appropriate decorum. One match programme stated: 'It is un-Irish to Boo and you should realise that all it achieves is to arouse the worst instincts in your own team. Silent contempt for the offender is more effective. The referee is selected for his honesty and integrity and his knowledge of the Playing Rules – but he is human. Did you ever make a mistake?'[22] In another match programme it

Cork and Louth parade before the 1957 All-Ireland final. Note that the Long Stand had been demolished with just the commentary box and the Hogan Stand in view.

was stated: 'Play the game is a motto that should apply to spectators as much as to players. The one-eyed spectator can be a nuisance to everybody around him. He is the supporter who sees only one side of everything – his own side … You will find this wholly unreasonable crank at every match. There is no excuse for the abusive attitude towards referees that is sometimes heard …'[23]

The 1957 finals were the last to be played in what would be the old Croke Park. The hurling final was a classic encounter between Kilkenny and Waterford. The parade before the match was notable for the addition of Hollywood actor John Gregson into the Kilkenny line-out during the parade around the field. The parade was filmed as part of the movie *Rooney* about a Dublin bin-man who fell in love with his landlady's daughter. In one of the most exciting finals Kilkenny, who had led by five points in the first half, found themselves behind by two goals half way through the second half. They made an astounding comeback in 'one of the most agonisingly thrilling finals ever played'. Taking the last three scores in the match (two goals and a point) Kilkenny won the match by a point, 4-10 to 3-12.

On 22 September 1957 the football final was played between Louth and Cork. Louth had last played in a final at the GAA's main venue when they met Kerry in the two games it took to decide the Croke Cup final in 1913. It was those matches that had provided the funds for the purchase

Lynn Dunlea

FORMER CORK CAMOGIE PLAYER AND WINNER OF FOUR
ALL-IRELAND MEDALS

I was often in Croke Park supporting all kinds of Cork teams before I went to play there. I would say that it was overwhelming as a child but I would not swap being there for anything. I came there as a member of the Cork camogie team to play against Galway in the final of 1993. We togged out that day in the old dressing rooms under the Hogan Stand and the feeling was terrific as we marched around behind the Artane Band. I had a good look up at the stands and I could pick out my friends and family members.

I played in the next four finals and won three of them with the only loss coming in 1996 when Galway were too good for us. By then we were in the new dressing rooms under the Cusack and they are simply amazing. I think the idea of having an Astro-turf area for practice before going out is a brilliant one and I used it a lot.

I did not bother looking up at the Stands after the '93 match – better to concentrate on the game. After that I became a television commentator and was able to see the whole arena. It was strange to be talking on the telly about my sister Stephanie.

There is no place like Croke Park.

New Hogan Stand, Croke Park.

STRUCTURAL STEELWORK
for the new
HOGAN STAND

Smith & Pearson Ltd., fabricated and erected the steelwork for the Long Stand and Hogan Stand in 1924 ; in 1938 the Cusack Stand and in 1954 the Railway End Stand. Now in 1959 Smith & Pearson Ltd., are proud to have fabricated and erected the steelwork for the New Hogan Stand. Justifiable pride in the continued expansion of Croke Park and the continued confidence of the G.A.A. in their reliability and sound workmanship.

NEWCOMEN WORKS, DUBLIN, PHONE 45914

An advertisement showing the steelwork used in the construction of the Hogan Stand.

of Jones' Road. Appropriately it was the Louth captain Dermot O'Brien who was last to walk up the steps of the old Hogan Stand to receive the trophy. Later that week T. McInerney and Sons began to dismantle the old Hogan Stand for reassembling at the Gaelic Grounds in Limerick.[24] During this development the Long and Corner stands were demolished, as was the commentary booth that had been home to Micheál O'Hehir.

THE NEW HOGAN STAND

On 7 June 1959 the new Hogan Stand was officially opened to celebrate the seventy-fifth anniversary of the founding of the GAA. Over 900 All-Ireland medal winners were specially invited to the ceremony. The Hogan Stand now ran the full length of the field with a capacity of 16,000 seats in its two tiers. For its time the stand was an engineering achievement. The new Hogan was over 500 feet long. It was made from 700 tons of steel reinforcing bars that if laid end-to-end would have run from Dublin to Shannon Airport. There were 350 tons of structural steel and 6,000 cubic yards of concrete. The new Hogan was built with just three beams supporting its cantilevered roof. This was a significant improvement on the Cusack Stand

Fans suffer in the elements on a terrace in Croke Park.

The programme cover for the events opening the new Hogan Stand in June 1959.

Seats being hoisted into the Hogan Stand.

Test loading of the new Hogan Stand in 1959.

Jim Whelan

FORMER PUBLIC RELATIONS MANAGER OF COCA COLA AND WICKLOW SUPPORTER

My father Peter served as a member of the Leinster Council for thirty years and he brought me to Croke Park fairly often when I was young. My earliest memories of Croke Park would be of Railway Cup days, especially when the Leinster Football team would be in action. The early 1950s were particularly good when Leinster won four Railway Cups in a row – 1952, '53, '54 and '55. I was present for all four and they were particularly pleasing for Wicklow people. The reason was the presence of Wicklow players on the Leinster teams at a time when football was strong in several counties. Gerry O'Reilly and Jim Rogers gathered a huge reputation from Railway Cup participation and the St Patrick's Day finals were always big occasions. A crowd in excess of 30,000 was commonplace and there was great loyalty to provinces in those days. Gerry O'Reilly was at right half-back on the winning team of '52 and the other Wicklow man, Jim Rogers, was sited at midfield. Leinster beat a team of Munster stars that year. It is a measure of the consistency of the Wicklow duo that they occupied the same positions on the winning teams of the following two years beating Munster again in '53 and Connacht in '54.

The popular O'Reilly, who played a vigorous, flamboyant style of football was an absentee from the winning team of 1955 but Garda Rogers was still on midfield duty. However, Wicklow supplied the centre-back that year in the person of Jim Fitzpatrick. Later on, in the 1960s, the great Andy Phillips was Leinster's regular goalkeeper and he too had a great Croke Park reputation and won a Railway Cup medal in 1962, the day that Des Foley played on the winning hurling and football teams.

There was a custom that Wicklow followers brought a goat along dressed up in the county colours when the occasion was deemed important enough. I suppose the most disappointing day Wicklow ever experienced in Croke Park was the championship match with Meath in 1954. I remember it vividly and the great football Wicklow played when looking very likely winners for a long spell. Bill Delaney of Laois was the referee and nobody knows exactly how much extra time was allowed but in the end Meath were the winners. They won the All-Ireland later that year.

My favourite spot of ground as a spectator was the Hogan Stand but I did sample the atmosphere on Hill 16 and in a way it was like the 'Bank' at the famous Aughrim pitch. I was in the standing area under the old Cusack Stand for the All-Ireland football final of 1961 between Down and Offaly. That was the only time in history when the attendance at an All-Ireland final exceeded 90,000 and there was congestion under the Cusack. The wires between the area and the sideline were broken down and thousands got in on the grass to watch the match.

across the field whose numerous roof supports obstructed the views of spectators. The new 'Hogan' brought the seated capacity of the ground to 23,000 out of a total capacity of roughly 90,000, a very high ratio of seats to terracing for its time. There were also 5,000 square feet of office space.[25] The stand had cost £250,000, but £100,000 was raised in a ten-year All-Ireland ticket scheme which guaranteed a seat for every All-Ireland. A ten-year seat in the upper Hogan cost £11 and a seat in the Lower Hogan was £18. The transformation of Croke Park was complete. Only the playing pitch and the railway wall remained from the Croke Park of the early 1930s.

At the ceremony that officially opened the new stand the President of Ireland, Seán T. Ó Ceallaigh congratulated the GAA on behalf of 'Gaelic Ireland' but explained that 'I never played at Clonturk Park or Croke Park. Though I practiced and played hurling from my early youth I was never sufficiently accomplished in the game to be selected on a team to play in Croke Park' but had only played against 'fumblers like myself on the wide open spaces of the Phoenix Park'.[26] According to the GAA's Annual Report it was thought it would be 'fitting to recall the long years during which the nation lived in the shadows – which the colour and vitality of our games did much to dispel' so part of the day's events was 'The Pageant of the Flag' performed on the pitch. The pageant paid tribute to four generations of Irish patriots – the United Irishmen, the Fenians and those who took part in the Easter Rising and the War of Independence. The day's centrepiece was the delayed hurling Railway Cup final between Munster and Connacht. The match was a disappointment but was notable for the four goals and five points scored by the 38-year-old Christy Ring.

THE RECORD CROWD

The aim of the redevelopment of Croke Park had been to make the ground big enough to accommodate all those who wanted to watch the matches. Despite the opening of the new Hogan Stand the annual September ticket famine was not brought to an end. It seemed that there was no satisfying the hunger for tickets that were then small white, pink and yellow pieces of card 5 inches wide and 3 inches high. In 1960 there was an unprecedented demand by supporters of a hopeful Down team and a

Bridie Martin McGarry

FORMER KILKENNY CAMOGIE CAPTAIN AND WINNER OF NINE ALL-IRELANDS

I first played in Croke Park in 1969 for Presentation College, Kilkenny, against Terenure of Dublin in the Leinster Junior final. I think the game was played on a Saturday before a small attendance but that did not matter. It was great to be there.

I played for the Kilkenny senior team in the 1972 All-Ireland and what I remember most about it is the sight of the team in long yellow gym slips down to our ankles. We were well beaten by Cork the same day but we won our first All-Ireland two years later by beating Cork in a replay. We wore short skirts that day, the first team to do so and the new fashion spread after that.

We were regular visitors to the most famous sporting ground in Ireland from then on and my favourite position was centre-back.

I always liked playing the sod in Croke Park. It was impossible though to get the vastness of Croke Park out of the mind. Besides playing on the pitch it is very satisfying to watch a match being played there.

The view is perfect from all angles but my favourite spot is the lower deck of the Hogan Stand. You are near the action and it is even better for camogie since the rule was brought in that permitted the use of the full pitch and goals. The place has special memories for all those people privileged to have played there.

resurgent Kerry side. Before any tickets were made available to the public, allocations were distributed to thirty-nine county boards (thirty-two counties in Ireland and seven in Britain) with Down and Kerry and the minor finalists receiving an extra allocation. For the first time the forty senior players were given six complimentary tickets, 7,000 tickets were already reserved for long-term ticket holders and 300 were for the press. On the day 87,768 saw Down defeat Kerry to become the first northern team to win an All-Ireland. Archbishop Morris of Cashel presented Kevin Mussen of Down with the Sam Maguire trophy. The next day the Sam Maguire cup was brought north of the border for the first time.

In 1961 Down returned to Croke Park to play Offaly. Public interest was even greater than the previous year. On 7 September the GAA

Above: Action from the 1963 All-Ireland football final between Dublin and Galway.

Below: Action shot from the 1964 All-Ireland hurling final between Kilkenny and Tipperary.

27 - 9 - '70

ALL-IRELAND
FOOTBALL FINAL

SCOREBOARD
TERRACE 10/-

This ticket to be surrendered at Stile 3 or 4 Jones's Road

Seán Ó Síocháin
Ard Rúnaí.

Above: The Kerry and Meath teams line up before the start of the 1970 All-Ireland football final.

Left: A Croke Park match ticket from 1970.

announced that all stand tickets had gone; temporary staff were employed to return all excess applications for tickets. On the afternoon of Sunday 24 September the gates of Croke Park were closed at 1.45 on between 25,000 and 30,000 people. It was a remarkable day with a record crowd of 90,556. The day is regarded as one of the greatest in the history of the Association. Never before had so many people gathered in an Irish stadium for a sporting event. It is a record that is unlikely to be surpassed in a modern era of safety regulations, another notch in the achievement belt of the GAA.

Despite the fact that the day appeared to have everything – a 'glorious day, record crowd, two equal teams and a close finish', the atmosphere at Croke Park was curiously flat. One paper commented on a missing

Action shot from the 1970 All-Ireland camogie final.

'mysterious ingredient'.[27] Some put the blame on the crowd for not rising to the occasion. They were unusually quiet. However, it is likely the huge crowd may have been muted by their own size. They were jammed into every corner of Croke Park like never before. What is looked on as one of the greatest days in the history of the Association could just as easily have been its blackest day. A shuttle of ambulances ran between Croke Park and the Dublin hospitals carrying those who had fainted or were injured in the crush. Perhaps it was only the muted behaviour and self restraint of the crowd, wary of its own power in such circumstances, which saved the situation from possible catastrophe.

NEW CHALLENGES

The crowds of the 1940s, 1950s and early 1960s seemed to show that the GAA was on an ever-upward curve of popularity. Record attendance seemed to follow record attendance. In fact, it became newsworthy if a

Al McHugh

FORMER ASSISTANT GARDA COMMISSIONER

Croke Park was certainly a unique assignment for me. My association with the GAA goes back to when my father would bring me to matches in McCabe Park or Markievicz Park in Sligo. I think my first visit to Croke Park was in 1967 when I hitched up to see Mayo and Meath playing in the All-Ireland semi-final. That was the week I think John Morley had an appendix operation and he came on late in the game. As far as I can remember the power went and when the power came back I think Meath had scored two goals. I have a huge interest in the GAA. I have a great interest in the games, I understand the games and I understand the culture. There is a great delight in meeting people from the different counties involved in the GAA.

One occasion that stands out is the year Armagh won the All-Ireland the first time. The excitement and exuberance of their supporters before the match and then to see grown men crying with their children after they won – he had maybe travelled to matches for forty or fifty years before seeing his county win. It was a similar story with Tyrone the following year. They are special days to see counties that were in the wilderness or at least on the verge of wilderness for many years winning. I hope in my time at Croke Park that I will see the captain of a Mayo team walking up the steps to take the Sam Maguire. The best goal I saw was Padraig Brogan's goal in 1985 from the 21-yard line.

As emergency controller my spot during match games is with the event controller in our communications box but prior to the match I do intermingle with the different aspect of the policing. It is interesting to look at the reactions from the different captains as they motivate their players before they come on to the pitch, the excitement that often emanates from the dressing rooms onto the corridor outside would raise the adrenalin. I suppose for me the one spot I would pick before I head to the communications box is at the junction of what was the Nally and the Hogan Stand. I stand there for the national anthem and then I go about my business.

As the policeman in charge a huge atmosphere always came from the Hill and I'd have to say that certainly Dublin brought a sense of difference to the stadium on match days. The 10,000 jubilant supporters, including three of my own kids, often would be there.

Above: The New York Police Band perform at Croke Park in 1971.

Right: Micheál O'Hehir, the voice of Gaelic games for many years, at Croke Park.

Joe Rock

MATCH DAY STAFF

My father was the first member of the Rock family to work at Croke Park. My father died in 1972 and he had been associated with Croke Park for most of his eighty-seven years. My eldest brother John used to be caretaker at Croke Park and also worked the scoreboard. My other brothers, Charlie and Christie, worked as stiles-men. Willie Rock was also a stilesman and his son Barney later played for Dublin.

My father was close with 'Chicky' Curran and the rest of the Currans. They all became a sort of family. And, of course, Paddy O'Keeffe who held my father in very high esteem. It was a three-part unit – my father, Chicky Curran and Paddy O'Keeffe.

From the age of six or seven I used to accompany my father to Croke Park. When I was eight I was given my first job by Chicky Curran. It was to pick up the orange and lemon skins at the end of half-time (at the time the teams never came off the pitch at half-time). That job lasted, I suppose, four or five years and then I progressed into the dressing rooms. The first job I got was in the dressing room underneath the old corner stand.

We used to have Ceilis underneath that old Hogan Stand on a Sunday night. It was a great attraction. There used to be spot prizes and my father won a couple of tea sets – we still have those tea sets up in the house. There were plenty of women there. Great nights we had there, wonderful times, great thoughts, great memories.

In the old days the grass on the pitch was cut with a pony. The pony used to pull this little grass mowing machine and Chicky Curran used to do all the cutting and when the cutting would be done he would bring the pony back in and he'd let it out maybe on the grass. We used to have to look after the horse. One time the pony got sick during the night. Chicky went in the next morning and the pony was rolling in the stable. The first option he had was to come up to my father and get him to see what the problem was. So father went down and the pony had sort of a colic. So my father had to go down and 'drench' him. We'd drench him with ginger beer and half a pound of ginger. We'd get the handle of a shovel with a piece of rope at the end of it and we used to tie it to the bottom jaw of the horse and open up his mouth by pulling down on the rope and put the bottle down his neck and he'd have to swallow it. We'd throw it down its neck and he'd release the wind and he'd get better.

On All-Ireland days my father would wear a bowler hat for the occasion. One of my father's jobs was to present the ball to the referee before the finals. We used to mind the balls in the house and the fact was he would never sleep at night thinking that somebody might break in and they'd get the balls. He'd be awake all night thinking, would they be safe?

The only player my father ever hated seeing play was Eddie Keher. Eddie Keher hit the ball so hard that he often used to hit it over the railway wall. My father used to say 'oh there's another one gone, there's another one gone'. He used to say to himself, 'Eddie Keher, for God's sake, spare the balls'.

I have good memories when the Offaly people would come up to Croke Park and Father Magee and some other priests would come in to their dressing room before they went out to play the match and he'd put them all kneeling down. He'd drown them with holy water and he used to laugh at me when all the blessing was over.

Another memory is of Pat Spillane complaining about the tacks coming up from the old wooden floor in the changing room. He said they were sticking up into his feet and asked me to hammer them down. 'Now,' says I, 'you're not in your granny's now.'

I'm down there nearly eighty years working. I've seen all good changes. I've very good memories I have of Croke Park. Hopefully that will carry on.

major game at Croke Park did not attract a record or near record crowd. However, it was in the 1960s that the GAA faced its most serious challenge since the difficulties of the 1890s. These challenges were not specific to the GAA, yet in many ways they undermined the very foundations of the Association. Although the strength of the Association could not be accurately measured by attendances at headquarters one indicator of the impact of new circumstances was a decline in All-Ireland attendances at Croke Park. In the 1950s the average attendance at a football final was over 75,000 and hurling finals averaged over 71,000. In the 1960s these figures fell to 68,800 and 69,500 respectively.

In the 1960s Ireland began the process of modernisation. During the decade living standards rose by 50 per cent, leading to increased choice. The rural economy was in decline (agricultural employment fell from 379,000 to 273,000) and Ireland was becoming increasingly urbanised. New ideas challenged traditional views. These changes in society confronted the GAA with a number of issues. Increasing income and choice led to more options for people to pursue in their leisure time. Urbanisation threatened to undermine a largely rural-based Association. New attitudes that challenged the social conservatism in Ireland were also a threat to an Association that had identified itself with the twin pillars of Church and State.

One major factor affecting GAA attendances was the opening of the Irish national television station, Télefís Éireann, in 1961. It was given much of the blame for the declining attendances. The first GAA matches to be televised were the Down All-Irelands of 1960 and 1961 when UTV and BBC Northern Ireland showed delayed coverage and highlights. In 1962 the GAA, aware of the potential threats posed by the new media but also conscious that the Association should have a pre-eminent position in the new window on the Irish world, agreed to have the All-Ireland semi-finals and finals televised live by the national station. To help the fledgling station they initially only charged a nominal fee to broadcast their games. On 6 August 1962 the first game to be broadcast live was the Kerry-Dublin football semi-final played at Croke Park. The first final screened was the 1962 hurling final between Tipperary and Wexford. Irish people soon became used to seeing Gaelic games on television. At the time of the 1966 hurling final the media net was cast wide at home and abroad. Télfís Éireann and BBC Northern Ireland showed the game live while the worldwide Irish community was brought to Croke Park through the live

A section of the large crowd at the 1962 All-Ireland hurling final.

relay of radio broadcasts to Toronto, Boston, New York, San Francisco, Chicago and Los Angeles (the missionaries were still being catered for by Radio Brazzaville). Later in the month the American Broadcasting Company's programme, *Wide World of Sport,* re-broadcast the hurling final between Cork and Kilkenny – the first time an Irish sporting event was shown on television in colour.[28]

At the same time as these general changes in Irish society it was commented upon by many that the standard of play in Gaelic games had declined. It was a time when soccer began to make its presence felt. Soccer was boosted significantly by the televising of the soccer World Cups of 1966 (held in England) and 1970 (featuring the great Brazilian team including Pelé).

While the GAA was facing all these challenges in the 1960s the games themselves seemed to be going through a poor patch. It was not a great decade for the national games. Of course, supporters of the hurlers of Tipperary who dominated hurling in the 1960s (they competed in seven of the ten finals, winning four of them), or the footballers of Galway who won three All-Irelands in a row from 1964–1966 would regard it as a golden era.

There were two distinct trends. One was a decline in the number of teams competing for the major honours. In the 1950s ten teams appeared in the football finals. In the 1960s this fell to eight. The problem was even more acute in hurling with eight teams competing in the 1950s finals as compared to five teams competing in the 1960s finals. Just as worrying was what was perceived as a general decline in the spectacle the matches provided. There was a marked increase in frees and the percentage of scores that came from frees. In the football All-Irelands between 1964 and 1970 there was on average a free every two minutes. In the hurling finals frees were coming every eighty seconds. Scores from frees could account for 50 per cent of scores in a hurling final and as high as 65 per cent in a football final.[29] While the hurling finals of the 1950s produced 51 goals and 187 points the 1960s saw 48 goals and 225 points. In football the situation was considerably worse with the finals of the 1960s producing just 16 goals and 185 points as compared to 26 goals and 164 points in the finals of the previous decade.

Indicative of this state of affairs was the 1965 football final featuring Galway and Kerry. It was described by journalist Mick Dunne as an

Front row, from left, Taoiseach Sean Lemass, Prince Rainier and Princess Grace of Monaco and Mrs Lemass, watching the 1963 All-Ireland hurling final between Kilkenny and Waterford.

embarrassment which 'instead of showing all that is best in the most popular of our national games exhibited all that is worst in it. It showed that at its worst it can be over-roughly and pettily contested and that it can be productive of jagged, disruptive play lacking in continuity'.[30] There were, of course, exceptions to the trends. One of these was the 1963 hurling final between Kilkenny and Waterford. In the VIP seats that day were Princess Grace and Prince Rainier of Monaco. The match produced the highest scoring final on record. Kilkenny beat Waterford 4-17 to 6-8. It was 'an

Dignitaries at the 1974 All-Ireland hurling final include: front row from left, Archbishop Morris, President Childers, Mrs Childers, Donal Keenan (President of the GAA), Mrs Cosgrave and An Taoiseach, Liam Cosgrave.

hour of bewildering breathtaking hurling, played at a staggering pace, super-charged with high drama and nerve-wracking tension and radiant with the most splendid and spectacular scores'.[31] Princess Grace commented that it was 'fast, almost too exciting, it's marvellous'.[32]

The facilities at Croke Park played their own part in the general decline. Croke Park had been re-built between 1949 and 1959. This was by no means a classic era in Irish architecture or design. Its rudimentary constructions aged quickly while general standards demanded by an increasingly sophisticated public meant that what had once seemed ultra modern had become dated. Decades later one person recalled that in the 1970s, while Croke Park was 'utterly magical', it 'was a gum-blackened, down on its luck tangle of metal, stone and moisture … gaunt, mildewed and basic. A place immune to market research … symptomatic of a

Séamus Darby's last-minute goal to win the 1982 All-Ireland for Offaly and deny Kerry the five-in-a-row.

national mindset. We lacked ambition and self-confidence'.[33] In 1971 a report carried out by the GAA as part of the McNamee Commission proposed a number of changes at Croke Park. For the first time the GAA recognised that it needed to make a conscious and determined effort 'to woo the spectator … It is therefore vital to think of an attendance at a match not as a statistic or a conglomerate mass of people, but as a grouping of individual spectators.'[34] That the changes envisaged were basic underlined just how far behind the main stadium of the GAA had fallen behind the expectations of the times. Among the suggestions for Croke Park was that it should have a first-class amplifications system, it should make the maximum use of colour when repainting or redecorating areas, the toilet accommodation should be modernised, professional catering should be used on match days, the 'feasibility' of using buses to convey teams engaged in

Action from the 1980 All-Ireland hurling final between Galway and Limerick.

Tom Cheasty

FORMER WATERFORD HURLER AND WINNER OF ALL-IRELAND MEDAL IN 1957

Waterford did not get to Croke Park too often in my young days and I thought it was a great honour for the county and my club Ballyduff when I was selected on the 'Rest of Ireland Team' to play there in 1956. We were playing against the Ireland team and I started on the 40 and marked Billy Rackard.

I loved the sod from the minute I stepped on it and I thought it was easier to play on than Thurles. Thurles used to be very fast especially in dry summer weather. I never minded playing on Billy Rackard but I was not making a great fist of it that day and I was shifted into the corner after a while. The man marking me there was Billy's brother Bobby and it didn't look good for me when I was told to move in. But it worked well in the end and I scored three goals off Bobby. No wonder I liked Croke Park forevermore.

I did not think I would get a chance to get back there so soon again but we won the Munster championship of '57 and that gave us a real right to be there. The All-Ireland semi-final against Galway was the start of many visits – we won that easily and then we had a very exciting final with Kilkenny and were only beaten by a point. I was very nervy before that match but it was not the crowd that made me that way. I was very fit but I would like if there was some place where I could warm up a bit. It was funny to see Kilkenny with sixteen players in the parade – John Gregson, the actor, walked around and it was filmed for the film *Rooney*. They say he wanted to march with us but he was not allowed anyway.

Leaving Croke Park that day I wondered would I ever get back but it happened again in 1959 and this time luck was with us – we beat Kilkenny in a replay of the All-Ireland final. It was a big day for Waterford people and I scored 2-2 in that replay. I was lucky from then on and won three Railway Cup medals on my favourite pitch – 1960, '61, and '63. And we were back again in September of '63 to play in another All-Ireland final against Kilkenny. They won by three points and we had no complaints – the experience of playing in four All-Ireland finals between 1957 and '63 was something I will never forget.

All-Ireland semi-finals and finals from their hotels in Dublin right into Croke Park should be examined and that after matches teams should meet for light refreshments in the Hogan Stand.[35]

In the 1970s Croke Park witnessed some of its most memorable football encounters. The teams of Kerry and Dublin and their rivalry defined the decade. The Dublin team were moulded by Kevin Heffernan and attracted a huge following in the capital. The Dublin team included Paddy Cullen, Gay O'Driscoll, Robbie Kelleher, Brian Mullins, Tony Hanahoe, Anton O'Toole and Jimmy Keaveney. Although Hill 16 had long been a favourite for Dublin people the blue of the Dublin supporter came to define Hill 16 during the 1970s and has since provided Croke Park with some of its most memorable images. Kevin Moran later put the atmosphere generated by the success of the Dublin team during this era into perspective. Moran had played for Dublin during this era but went to England to pursue a soccer career. Having played in the English first division, European competitions and the FA Cup he said that the atmosphere in Dublin at the time was only eclipsed during Italia '90.

In 1974 Dublin beat Galway to win their first All-Ireland since 1963. In the 1975 semi-final Dublin lost to a young Kerry side. It was the beginning of a series of truly remarkable encounters. In 1976 Dublin came back and beat Kerry in the final with a blistering display. In the 1977 semi-final against Kerry the two teams were level four times in the second-half. Kerry then took the lead but two Dublin goals sealed victory. This game is regarded by many as the greatest game of football ever played. In 1978 Dublin lost to Kerry in the final. In 1979 Kerry defeated Dublin again by a score of 3-13 to 1-8. The Dublin star was on the wane while Kerry had just begun a brilliant four-in-a-row.

The Kerry teams of 1978-82 boasted outstanding players in nearly every position – Charlie Nelligan, Ger Power, Jack O'Shea, Páidí Ó Sé, Eoin Liston, John Egan, 'Ogie' Moran, Mikey Sheehy and Pat Spillane. In 1979 Kerry again defeated Dublin. In 1980 they were hot favourites against Roscommon. In a game marred by sixty-four frees Kerry won by three points. Back to Croke Park for the 1981 final they faced an ever-improving Offaly side. Kerry won 1-12 to 1-8 and became only the third team in the history of the games to win four consecutive football All-Irelands (the others in football were the Wexford team of 1915–1918 and the Kerry team of 1929–1932, while Cork had won four-in-a-row in hurling in the years 1941–44). With the weight of expectation on Kerry, Offaly led at half-time. Kerry then dominated much of the second half. With five minutes to go they were leading by four points and the five-in-a-row seemed in their grasp. However, two points from frees brought Offaly back into contention. Then a dramatic goal from Offaly substitute Séamus Darby snatched victory from Kerry – pure sporting drama.

CHAPTER FIVE
1983-2013

All-Ireland hurling final between Clare and Kilkenny, 2002.

The football final of 1983 has gone down as one of the most bad-tempered finals in All-Ireland history. Dublin beat Galway on a cold and blustery day that was punctuated with heavy, squally showers. It was Galway's first final since losing to Dublin in 1974 and Dublin's first since they had lost to Kerry in 1979. By the end of the match Dublin had been reduced to twelve players – they were dubbed both the 'Dirty Dozen' and the 'Twelve Apostles' – and Galway had been reduced to fourteen. It was certainly no classic, but the final was a turning point in the history of Croke Park as it was from incidents at this match that the idea of rebuilding the modern Croke Park was first raised as a serious and burning issue.

The crowd on the day was a large one by any standards. It was one of the last finals at which it was possible to walk up to Croke Park on the day of a match and pay at the turnstile for admission to one of the terraces. That day 71,988 paid into Croke Park. This was about the official capacity of the ground – since 1966 there had been only three larger attendances. The size of the crowd was a major factor but there was another less tangible factor involved. Crowd behaviour is a curious phenomenon. They can generate their own collective mood and it was noticed on the day that the crowd were in poor form – narky, grumpy, cantankerous. Trouble was not inevitable but there was an unhealthy atmosphere around the ground.

There were a number of problems. While there was overcrowding on the Canal End the main trouble on the day centred on Hill 16. At the time the Hill was often the site of violent scenes caused by a thug element – Gardaí with batons and a parting in the sea of Dublin blue was a fairly common sight in one corner of the terrace. Fans who were crammed onto the terrace broke through a gap in the fence (which had been left by construction works) that separated the Cusack Stand from the Hill. They sat in empty seats in the partially-covered lower deck and some forced people out of their seats. There were a number of confrontations and scuffles. On the other side of the Hill missiles were being thrown from the terrace into the Nally Stand where OAPs and students were sitting. Finally, at the end of the match, the most serious incident occurred. Behind the Hill was a walkway with a single set of concrete steps going to ground level. On either side of the stairs were steep grassy banks. Normally the crowd would wait to go down the stairs, or slowly make their way down the slope. On this occasion people slid at speed down the wet banks, often before the people who had gone before them were

Dublin celebrates lifting the Sam Maguire trophy in 1983.

able to move away. It was reported that it was a miracle people had not been killed as the crowd exited the ground at the rear of Hill 16. Fatalities were only avoided by the slimmest of margins and the intervention of stewards and Gardaí.

The events of that day focused the thoughts of the GAA Director General, Liam Mulvihill, on the safety of spectators at Croke Park. The role of the Director General (formerly General Secretary) has been crucial to the Association because it provides continuity between the various presidents whose term lasts just three years. The men in this post have played key roles in the various phases of modernisation at Croke Park. Mulvihill was only the GAA's third Director General since Luke O'Toole's death in 1929. The latest redevelopment of Croke Park took place during the terms of seven presidents but it is Mulvihill's influence that is seen in most of the files relating to the stadium and is evident in all aspects of the new Croke Park. Born in Kenagh, Longford, in 1945 Mulvihill was educated at St Mel's College, Longford. He then went on to St Patrick's Training College, Drumcondra. He became a primary school teacher and at the age of twenty-seven was appointed schools inspector. He played football at under-21 and senior level for Longford. At the age of twenty-four Mulvihill was appointed Chairman of the Longford County Board. In 1979, when he was thirty-four, he was appointed to the post of Director General of the GAA. He was the youngest person to have held the post.

PREPARING FOR A NEW STADIUM

The original plan for Croke Park focused on the redesign of Hill 16 where the trouble had been in 1983. Initiated under GAA President Paddy Buggy, the reconstruction of the Hill was completed in 1988. At the same time that the Hill 16 project was being carried out the rest of the ground was looked at. The GAA's aim was for a capacity of 90,000. The initial idea was for a somewhat unambitious engineering driven redevelopment. This involved the addition of a third tier to the Hogan Stand – provision for another tier had been made during its construction in the 1950s[1] – with the Cusack Stand being replaced by a mirror image of the now larger Hogan. Another roofed tier of seating was to be added to the Canal End.

The site of Hill 16 after its demolition in 1987.

This plan was presented to a meeting of Central Council when, in what turned out to be an important intervention, Ger McKenna of Kerry suggested that outside experts be consulted. Liam Mulvihill turned to Geraint John, stadium adviser to the British Sports Council, for advice. John strongly advised that the GAA commission a master plan for the redevelopment. He also gave a list of firms to contact. After a whittling down process two firms, HOK (one of the largest architectural firms in the world) and Lobb (a sports specialist) were interviewed. They came from completely opposite ends of the spectrum of stadium design – one favoured stands, the other bowl stadiums, one favoured steps, the other ramps, one favoured a high corporate element, the other basic facilities. While GAA President Dowling favoured Lobb, Mulvihill favoured HOK. The classic compromise was reached when the two companies were asked to work together on producing a master plan for the new GAA headquarters. It was a curious beginning to a relationship that would see HOK and Lobb merge and go on to design some of the world's great stadiums including Stadium Australia (venue for the 2000 Olympics) and Wembley Stadium.

In 1989 the GAA embarked on perhaps its most ambitious project since its foundation. More than any other previous development of Croke Park this vision was breathtaking in its scale. The president of the GAA at the time was Peter Quinn. It was certainly a case of the right man in the right place. Original estimates put the cost of the new Croke Park in the region of £115 million. A self-made businessman, Quinn was not afraid of the figures involved. In addition Quinn, in his profession as an economics advisor, was held in high regard in the financial community. This was particularly important when packages were being discussed with financial institutions.

The other presidents who held office during the redevelopment of Croke Park were Mick Loftus, John Dowling, Jack Boothman, Joe McDonagh, Sean McCague and Sean Kelly. Each has had to grapple with the stadium issue during one or more of its phases. None of these men were of an ideal background for the type of project involved – they were teachers, veterinary surgeons, local authority officers, etc. As president they not only had to lead the largest sporting organisation in the country but they also had to undertake the redevelopment of the association's most important physical asset that was also a national icon. This also meant leading the largest single construction project in the history of the state.

Ray McManus

SPORTSFILE PHOTOGRAPHIC AGENCY

I 've been going to Croke Park for more than thirty years. Of all the stadiums I've been in around the world the noise at Croke Park is probably the loudest – the Clare or Kilkenny roar is hardly surpassed.

As a photographer I used to sit at the Hogan/Canal corner. Then I changed positions each match. Now I sit at the Hill/Cusack at the white flag and never move. Most goals I believe are scored at that end. It's probably because when the sun shines it shines into the goalkeeper's eyes. But I always sit in that one spot. If it happens there I get it, if it happens anywhere else, well, that's tough.

The result of a match is usually totally insignificant to me. Except when Dublin is playing and then it is sacrosanct.

I used to live on Clonliffe Road and my first important memory of Croke Park was when I was at the top of the Cusack Stand watching the Muhammad Ali fight. That was some memorable occasion. At the time I was a furniture salesman. When I became unemployed I turned my hobby of photography into my job.

The best picture I ever took was over twenty-five years ago. I got a phone call one afternoon from the *Evening Herald* to go to Croke Park to take a picture of a schools' final. I got the call at 2.15 and the match had started at 2.00. At that time I had an office in Great Denmark Street so I was only about 500 yards away from it. So I got up and got the car parked. When I got in the match was over but I got one of the best pictures that I ever got of a small child. He'd just conceded about seven or eight goals and he was in tears walking off the pitch. It made the front page of the *Herald* the next day.

During the 2002 All-Ireland football final we took a picture of the entire Croke Park from the top of Hill 16. [This photograph was taken at precisely 3.29 when the Kerry team had taken up their positions and the Armagh team were in a final huddle. Flags were waving around the stadium. It later appeared in *A Season of Sundays*, 2002.] At the end of the match nobody usually goes onto the field and you can leave the cameras down. Of course, when Armagh won everybody ran onto the field including a local gouger who took a loan of this camera worth seven and a half grand. Thankfully I met him about a half an hour later. He was standing outside asking all the photographers outside the ground if they had taken any good pictures today. I copped on to what his coded message was and I later bought the camera back for €50.

The scale of the project undertaken can only be appreciated by following the process in outline.

The master plan produced by HOK/Lobb in consultation with the GAA was ready in the spring of 1990. It was an ideal document for an ideal world but it provided a development control document to guide the stadium's construction and Mulvihill called it the smartest thing they did. The most fundamental issue to be addressed by the master plan was the need for a new stadium. Croke Park as it existed was put under the spotlight cast by the Guide to Safety at Sports Grounds (1986) produced in the aftermath of the stadium disasters in England and Europe (the crowd disasters at Hillsborough and Bradford in England in which over 150 people had died showed the possible consequences of continuing to use what were now antiquated structures). Like most other stadiums of its time Croke Park fell short of the new criteria.

On the most pressing issue of safety there was a catalogue of short-comings. Croke Park had an insufficient number of emergency exits, they were not clearly marked, there was no lighting for the emergency exits, the exits had no panic bolts and were reliant on a steward being present to open them, should one of these be blocked there were no easily accessible alternative emergency exits and there was no assembly point for spectators in the event of an evacuation of the stadium. While the Canal and Hogan areas fell short of modern standards, the most pressing area was identified as the Cusack Stand. Built in 1938 it was close to the end of its safe lifetime and the roof was considered to be 'in an advanced state of dilapidation'. Access to and egress from the Cusack Stand was through a passageway just 4.5 metres wide – far too narrow for its 14,000-person capacity.

In terms of general circulation there was virtually no separation of the stadium's users – players' and officials' dressing rooms were located off the main public concourse in the Hogan, machine rooms, plant rooms, work-shops and field maintenance storage areas were all located off the main concourse area with minimal security. Emergency and other vehicles were required to use the same routes as spectators. The number of people entering the stadium was not adequately controlled with turnstile operators occasionally accepting money at the turnstiles without authorisation, children being lifted over the stiles (in the time-honoured Croke Park tradition) and the machinery at the turnstiles manipulated to allow more than one person to pass through at a time.

An aerial view of the old Croke Park.

At a more general level only a minority of seats at Croke Park had adequate views. Spectators in the front rows had to stand to see all the action thus forcing those behind to stand. When the ball travelled above a certain height viewing was very limited for many seats. As a result very few spectators were able to follow a game in its entirety without having to stand at some time. The number of toilets was insufficient and those that existed were sub-standard. There were a minimal number of food outlets. The commercial possibilities presented by crowds of over 70,000 were very much under exploited.[2]

Under such a weight of evidence the GAA was faced with no choice but to completely rebuild its headquarters.

In 1989 the firm Gilroy McMahon was appointed executive architects to the project. A design team was assembled to put the master plan concepts into steel and concrete in Dublin 3. This design team consisted of Liam Mulvihill, Des McMahon of Gilroy McMahon, Chris Gogarty and Greg Noonan of Seamus Monahan and Partners (project managers and quantity surveyors) and Liam Connolly of J.V. Tierney. The design team liaised with the master plan team that acted as a 'Peer Review Group'. The team looked to other stadiums for guidance. As part of the research for the project the design team made visits to a number of European and American stadiums. The European ones included Wembley and Twickenham in England, the Nou Camp and Bernabeau in Spain and the Stadium of Light in Portugal. Among the American stadiums visited were Joe Robby Stadium (Miami), Camden Yards (Baltimore), Tampa Stadium (Florida), Mile High Stadium (Denver), Coors Field (Denver), the Cleveland Browns stadium, Giants Stadium (New Jersey) and Kansas City's Arrowhead Stadium. (During the course of the whole project formal and informal trips to other stadiums around the world continued to influence the evolving Croke Park. One particularly influential trip was made in 1991 as the initial design stage was coming to an end. This was a five-day whistle-stop tour of Italian stadiums that had been built for the World Cup. In train carriages between Italian cities the last architectural touches, inspired by Italian design, were put to the blueprints for Croke Park.)

During the research the American model of stadium emerged as the most relevant – particularly influential were Joe Robby Stadium in Miami and Giants Stadium where Ireland would play Italy in the 1994 soccer World Cup. The basic distinction between the European and American stadiums was that most European ones were either publicly owned or received considerable public funding. The American ones were privately built with one eye fixed firmly on the issue of finance. Croke Park was to be largely funded out of the association's own purse and, although significant State aid was to be forthcoming at various stages of the project, the reality of having to fund its own development resulted in what can be described as 'marketing-generated architecture'. The new Croke Park Stadium would be divided horizontally in what was basically one structure, instead of vertically in individual stands, which had been the tradition. The lower and upper levels were for general admission. The middle third level was split between corporate boxes and premium seats (long-term tickets in a segregated area with bars and restaurants). Not surprisingly in an organisation like the GAA there was some unease at these commercial imperatives and it took two years for the membership to accept the concept (a number of motions were tabled at Congress to stop the corporate level being built). The reality was that the corporate boxes and premium seats, accounting for a small minority of the seats in the stadium, would go a significant way towards funding the rest of the stadium. No corporate boxes or premium seats would have meant no stadium.

The vital issues considered by HOK/Lobb in the master plan included the number of tiers in the stadium, the safety of players and spectators, the efficient construction of the stadium to maximise potential, reduce cost, provide a stadium suitable for Gaelic games and flexible enough to accommodate other events, increasing the ease of access and use of Croke Park for the public, capitalising on commercial possibilities – including long-term tickets and corporate boxes, provide a stadium design that had a sense of identity that would complement the image of the GAA (and Dublin). Other issues included ensuring the use of Irish materials, components and manufacturers where possible, an assessment of ground and subsoil conditions, main frame and structural considerations, roof design and construction, prefabrication and testing of structural elements, the control of appearance, cost and delivery dates, and the means of adequately dealing with the difficulty presented at the Canal End.

The governing rule of any stadium design is the concept of 'sightline'. It is the sightline that gives a spectator a good view of the field of play. There is a complex formula for discovering the optimal overall sightlines. Essentially it dictates that the farther you are away from the pitch the higher you have to be above the row in front to get an uninterrupted view of the pitch. There is also an optimal clearance between one person's eye and the top of the head of the person sitting in the row in front – the 'C-value'. However, there is a limit and the angle at the top should not exceed 35 degrees in order to avoid people getting the sensation that they are falling – the 'vertigo effect'. The basic concept of sightline is relatively simple. Transferring it into reality is not. It is influenced by the size of the field of play, the desired capacity for the stadium, the size of the site and other issues. One of the major issues for the GAA was if the person in the last row of seats in the upper deck would be able to see a hurley ball. Indicative of the extent to which people were committed to the project was GAA President John Dowling climbing to the very last row of the upper deck of Joe Robby Stadium to see a sliotar on the pitch. Dowling suffered from a severe fear of heights and five people had to help him down.

One of the key decisions to affect the overall design was the solution to the problem posed at the Canal End. The original proposal was for a H-frame construction – the usual stadium design. However, this limited the number of seats at the Canal End and, because of the sightlines, the pitch would have been shunted towards the Hill and this would have reduced capacity on the Hill also. The architectural solution to the problem was to borrow from a bridge-building technique and produce a Y-frame stadium – the first of its kind. This not only saved money but it allowed the Canal End to accommodate roughly 20,000 seats in the airspace outside the Croke Park ground area. The air rights above the railway and Royal Canal had to be bought from Iarnród Éireann and Duchas – the Heritage Service. Today most of the seats in the Canal End are actually outside of the area owned by the GAA.

Would there be an athletics track? No, but in the end the stadium was constructed in such a way that seats can be easily removed to accommodate the laying of an athletics track. Would there be a moat around the field? No. How would the stadium look? According to the architect Des McMahon, internally it had to be 'a place of excitement, vigour, harmony, safety and comfort'. Externally, according to McMahon, it would be a

What a vision! The model of the proposed Croke Park with, from left, Jim Dent of Seamus Monahan and Partners, Des McMahon of Gilroy McMahon, Liam Mulvihill, Director General, Kevin Kelly of Sisk, Peter Quinn, GAA President, and George Sisk of Sisk.

landmark building that would also blend to some degree with its surroundings. To lighten its look it was divided into layers with a main concourse level, then curtain walls of slate blue mirroring the roof-scape of the surrounding area, finished off by a quintessentially Irish top layer, 'cloud grey designed for maximum interaction with the sky'. The roof design was subjected to testing at the Department of Aerospace Engineering at the University of Bristol.

Literally thousands of decisions had to be made throughout the project. What type of turnstiles would be used and how many were needed? How many ticket windows? What colour would the stadium be? What kind of seats? How wide? Should they be hinged? How many vomitories (the delightful word used for the passageways connecting the seating area of the stand with the concourses) would there be? What was the desirable fire rating? Where should the media area be? What should be in the media area? Where would the presentation area be? Should the dressing rooms have warm-up areas? How many corporate boxes would there be? How many people should the boxes accommodate? Should there be telephones in the boxes? Should the outside seats have cup holders? Should access around the stadium be controlled by smart card technology? How much area should be given for storage? How much office space was needed and where would it be? Would there be any escalators or would it be all stairs and ramps? What about signage? What about bins? What about food and beverage concession areas? What about non-match-day business areas like conference rooms? All the time there was the difficulty of carrying out the work in a highly built-up area. Although the GAA placed a public relations firm between them and the local community, relations with sections of that community were strained on a number of occasions. However, the problems caused by construction ultimately led to closer co-operation with local residents.

Fundamental to the project was that the Cusack Stand area would be the first to be developed, as this was in the worst state of repair. One of the main restrictions on the development was the ground at the rear of the Cusack Stand that had been sold by Frank Dineen over eighty years previously to Belvedere College. Not owning the land severely limited the potential for the stadium's development and raised the question of the GAA moving its traditional headquarters to a greenfield site. Tough negotiations with the school took place and a hard deal was fought to buy back the land through the purchase of an alternative site for a Belvedere sportsfield at Clonliffe College. Once the purchase of the Belvedere land had been sorted it was all systems go for the new stadium.

On 2 February 1992 the original planning application for the redevelopment was lodged with Dublin Corporation. During the year the drawings of the stadium and a scale model were brought around the country for presentation to members of the association. This was mainly done with a view to selling ten-year stand tickets for All-Ireland finals to the clubs. Leading this travelling road-show were Peter Quinn, Liam Mulvihill, Des McMahon and Chris Gogarty. Although only a minority of clubs availed of the opportunity nearly all of the 4,500 term tickets were sold. Importantly the presentations went some way towards selling the concept of the stadium as a whole. In early 1992, in the Ceannaras building at Croke Park, Mulvihill saw a group of people approach the model of what the stadium would look like. After discussing the model in detail one of them asked the question, 'will it ever be built?' It was a valid question. The Ceannaras building in which they were standing had only been built in 1984 and it had taken the GAA three years to raise the necessary £750,000 for its construction. However, Mulvihill simply replied 'It has to be.' After the usual appeals An Bórd Pleanála granted planning permission on 9 March 1993. It was anticipated that work would be carried out in four phases over the next fifteen years.

CONSTRUCTION

The day after the 1993 All-Ireland football final, when Derry were making their way home with the Sam Maguire Cup, heavy machinery started to demolish the Cusack Stand. Two years later the new Cusack Stand opened for the first time for the 1995 Leinster football final. The stand was 180m long and 35m high with a seating capacity of 25,000 and 48 corporate boxes. The new Cusack had cost €44.3 million (including the purchase of lands from Belvedere College) but the cost of the stand had almost been completely covered by the sale of corporate boxes and premium seats.

One of the most remarkable achievements during the reconstruction of Croke Park was the huge amount of finance raised through the sale of premium seats and corporate boxes, particularly to the Irish business community. To lead this part of the project Dermot Power was seconded from the Bank of Ireland. Power's achievement was spectacular. The first test came with the Cusack Stand. Had the numbers not stacked up at the end of this phase the project may have come to a grinding halt. But the stand more or less broke even. This was in a large part due to Power's marketing (and the help of a £5 million government grant). His second test was how to sell the premium seats and corporate boxes in the less desirable Canal End. This problem was solved by selling the Hogan facilities first and putting the holders in the Canal while the Hogan was being constructed – thus providing a perfect showcase for the Canal.

On the day that the premium level was first opened in 1996 Power and Mulvihill hid near the lift area to eavesdrop on people's initial response. The common reaction they heard was, 'Oh, bloody hell' and 'Oh, Jesus'. The 'Wow!' factor was there. Power later recalled that by the time people left that day the attitude had become 'Jesus, don't we deserve it'.

Initially the new Cusack was known as the 'New Stand'. For a while the GAA considered the idea of abandoning the naming of stands altogether and to name the levels of the stadium instead. This may have made sense in terms of architecture – the stadium was essentially going to be one structure, not a number of different stands – but it did not make sense to the average supporter. Tradition prevailed and today the original names are in place ensuring a fantastic sense of historic continuity. This historic theme was reinforced in 1998 when the GAA Museum, celebrating the games and their history, was opened in the Cusack Stand while on the main concourse of the stand a Hall of Fame celebrates the greats of Gaelic games. The modern stadium was branded with tradition.

As a result of cost consideration and in order not to disturb the Croke Park match schedule, the construction was planned in phases. Each phase would start in the autumn/winter months of October–December with the demolition of part of the old ground. Then January–June would see a race to get as many seats available in time for the major games of the upcoming season. The usual deadline was a Leinster football semi-final or final. Amazingly, throughout the whole reconstruction, the GAA held its full schedule of matches at Croke Park.

Phase two began after the 1997 All-Irelands when the Canal End was demolished. This was by far the most complex part of the construction as it involved working over the railway and culverting the Royal Canal over a distance of 140 metres. Phase three began in October 1999 when the old Hogan was demolished. At the end of the All-Ireland football final between Meath and Cork, supporters prised seats from the stand to take home as souvenirs. In 2000, when the Canal End was opened, only the lower part of the Hogan had been built – a decapitated stand. The progress in constructing the stadium was as public as possible. There was a slow build up of anticipation leading to the completed stadium.

In the midst of the construction project, in early 2002, the pitch at Croke Park was stripped and a new pitch was laid for the first time since the 1920s. The turf upon which decades of sporting drama was played was consigned to the tip head. The new Croke Park pitch was a 'Desso' pitch. First introduced in England ten years previously, it had been used in a number of different stadiums including Huddersfield, Anfield, Villa Park and Upton Park. The pitch is named after the 30cm-long pieces of green polypropylene string, or Desso, which were stitched into the playing area

The beginning of the Canal Stand. Note the absence of the Royal Canal which had been culverted during construction work.

The architect's drawings for the Canal End at Croke Park. Note that the main part of the stand, including the railway, is outside Croke Park proper. Also note the Y-frame, the base of which is enclosed between the railway and the canal.

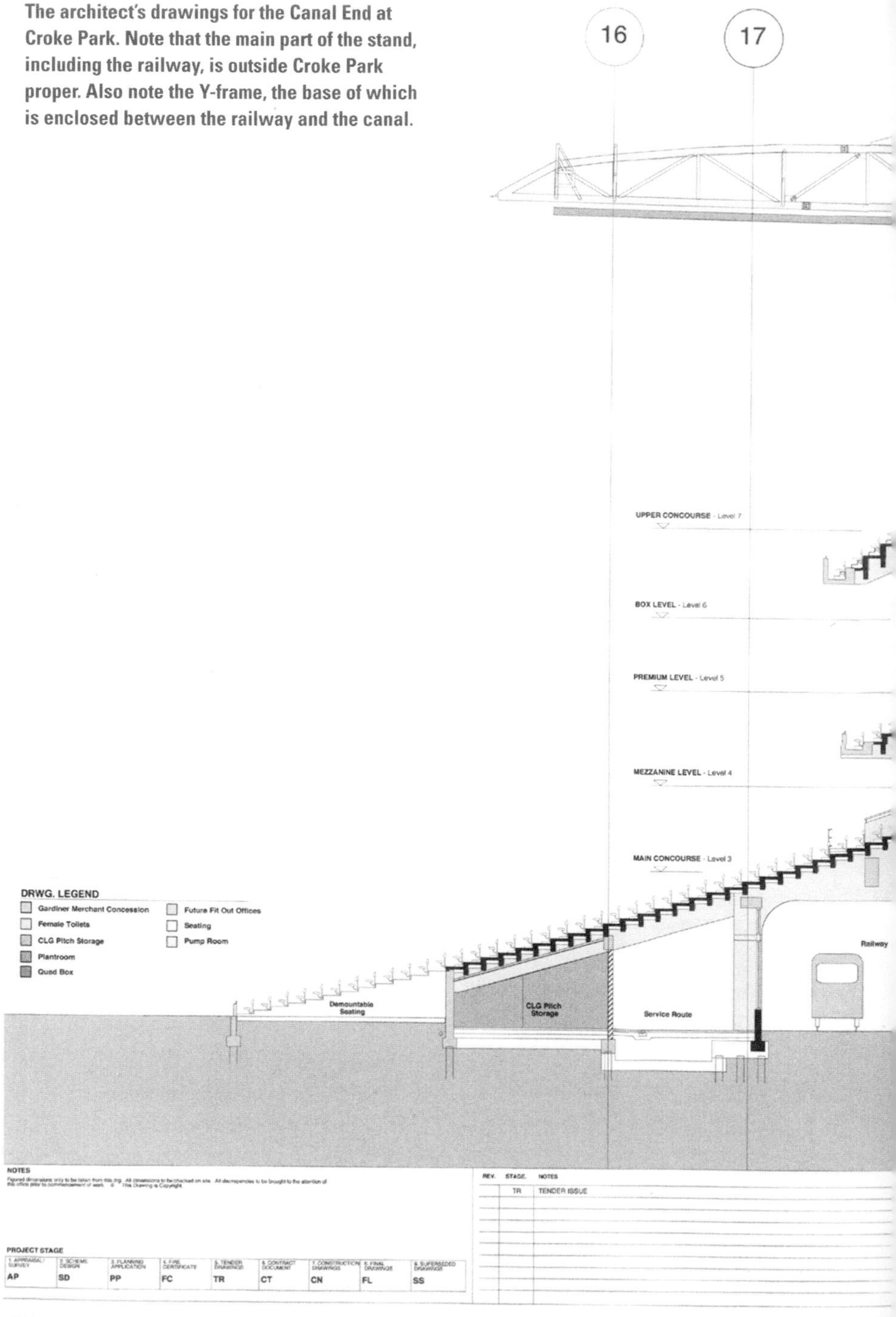

16   17

UPPER CONCOURSE - Level 7

BOX LEVEL - Level 6

PREMIUM LEVEL - Level 5

MEZZANINE LEVEL - Level 4

MAIN CONCOURSE - Level 3

Railway

DRWG. LEGEND
- Gardiner Merchant Concession
- Female Toilets
- CLG Pitch Storage
- Plantroom
- Quad Box
- Future Fit Out Offices
- Seating
- Pump Room

Demountable Seating

CLG Pitch Storage

Service Route

NOTES

REV.   STAGE.   NOTES
TR   TENDER ISSUE

PROJECT STAGE

1. APPRAISAL/ SURVEY	2. SCHEME DESIGN	3. PLANNING APPLICATION	4. FIRE CERTIFICATE	5. TENDER DRAWINGS	6. CONTRACT DOCUMENT	7. CONSTRUCTION DRAWINGS	8. FINAL DRAWINGS	9. SUPERSEDED DRAWINGS
AP	SD	PP	FC	TR	CT	CN	FL	SS

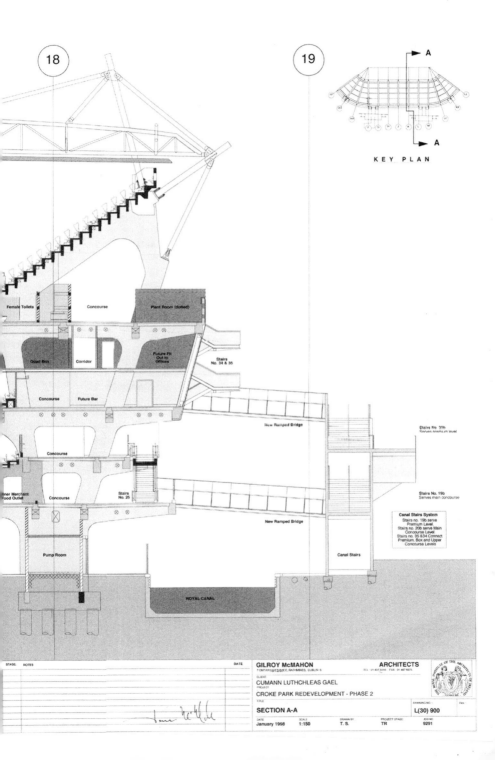

18

19

A

A

KEY PLAN

Female Toilets

Concourse

Plant Room (dotted)

Quad Bars

Corridor

Future Fit
Out to
Offices

Stairs
No. 34 & 35

Concourse

Future Bar

New Ramped Bridge

Concourse

Stairs No. 20b
Serves premium level

Concourse

Inner Merchant
Food Outlet

Concourse

Stairs
No. 25

New Ramped Bridge

Stairs No. 19b
Serves main concourse

Pump Room

Canal Stairs

Canal Stairs System
Stairs no. 19b serve
Premium Level.
Stairs no. 20b serve Main
Concourse Level.
Stairs no. 35 &34 Connect
Premium, Box and Upper
Concourse Levels

ROYAL CANAL

STAGE   NOTES   DATE

GILROY McMAHON   ARCHITECTS
7 ONTARIO TERRACE, RATHMINES, DUBLIN 6   TEL. 01 497 8099   FAX 01 497 6973

CLIENT
CUMANN LUTHCHLEAS GAEL
PROJECT
CROKE PARK REDEVELOPMENT - PHASE 2
TITLE
SECTION A-A

DRAWING NO.
L(30) 900

DATE
January 1998
SCALE
1:150
DRAWN BY
T. S.
PROJECT STAGE
TR
JOB NO.
9291

Declan Martin

FORMER ECONOMIC POLICY ADVISOR, DUBLIN CHAMBER OF COMMERCE

I grew up in Ballinasloe and even though I was only eight years of age at the time, I was brought along to Croke Park for the All-Ireland football final of 1963 between Galway and Dublin. I watched it from the Hogan Stand and was very disappointed when Dublin got the winning goal near the finish. I think I heard afterwards that Pat Donnellan was blaming himself for losing the match on account of wasting some of the possession he won during the game. But he and all the others, including my childhood hero Cyril Dunne, more than made up for it with a three-in-a-row that followed.

It was hurling for us from then on – my father Val had played for the county in the '40s and it was great to see the hurling team improve in the '70s. Tull Dunne was the man who got the tickets for us and I was always sent with the money in an envelope to collect them.

We were placed in a dilemma situation in the All-Ireland semi-final of 1980 when Galway lined out against Offaly because the Offaly goal-keeper, Damien Martin, was a cousin of ours. Galway won though and it was an extraordinary feeling when they won the final in September. It was almost like the impossible happening.

We had the same problem about Offaly in the All-Ireland final of 1981. I remember that it looked like another win for Galway until Offaly began to improve. I thought that our men had weathered the storm and started to come again with a strong attack towards the Railway Goal. Noel Lane hit well in search of a goal but our own cousin Damien brought off a fine save and I think it was the turning point in the second half. It brought the Liam MacCarthy Cup to Offaly for the first time.

The strangest feeling I ever experienced in Croke Park occurred at the All-Ireland hurling final of 1994. I was at the Canal End that day and whatever way the tickets were distributed that year it was practically all Limerick supporters in a sea of green. The game was flowing in their favour and they sang 'Limerick You're a Lady' at half-time. The mood was still a happy one until that shattering Offaly comeback led by Johnny Dooley's goal. The scene was transformed in a matter of minutes and the Canal End resembled a huge morgue with thousands of stunned and silent mourners. It emptied slowly and still in silence. For all the world it reminded me of a country funeral mass as I observed the steady stream of humanity with heads bowed trudge over the Canal Bridge.

Apart from my personal interest in Gaelic games, I also take a keen interest in Croke Park in terms of its importance to Dublin's economic life. Major sports events are recognised internationally as significant sources of revenue for the host city – since they bring in large numbers of people, who are spending money in local hotels, bars and restaurants as well as keeping the taxi drivers busy. Little wonder, for example, that American cities all seek to have a major league team in baseball or football, and that the team franchise owners often enter into bidding wars with cities to give them the best deal.

It is difficult to put a precise value on the economic contribution of Croke Park to Dublin but it is undoubtedly enormous.

In 2003, Croke Park attracted more than 1.3 million people to big matches, while visitor numbers to the Museum increased from 32,000 in 2001 to 45,000 in 2003. The greater number of these people are from outside Dublin, and bring considerable spending power with them on their visits to Dublin. Even more important, from an economic point of view, is the regular arrival of teams from Northern Ireland, since their supporters come from the sterling area, and they tend to be among the bigger spenders. The Tyrone v Armagh All-Ireland Final in 2003 is estimated to have brought some €12 million additional spending into Dublin over that weekend.

Croke Park has atmosphere. It is close to the city. It is modern and attractive. It is worth millions to Dublin.

Above: Liam Mulvihill saying goodbye to the last remnants of the old Hogan Stand.

Below: Sections of the Hogan Stand roof lie on the pitch in the background whilst, in the foreground, the pitch is dug up for relaying in spring 2002.

in a U-shape with tufts sticking up out of the ground. There was 86,000km of polypropylene used. Rye grass seed was then sewn and as the roots of the grass grew they wrapped around this stitching, thus providing great solidity to the pitch. In fact it is impossible to take a divot – thus increasing the difficulty of hurling's sideline cut. It is a sand based-pitch with 90 per cent sand and 10 per cent soil – when it was being constructed it looked like the Sahara Desert had blown in to Croke Park. Granules of foam is mixed with the free-draining soil. The pitch is cambered, with the centre of the pitch one foot higher than the sidelines to assist in drainage. Water is drained from the pitch by a double-wishbone network of pipes. Two pipes 600mm in diameter are the drainage pipes. There are seventy-six smaller pipes which feed into each of these two main pipes. The main pipes are connected to a huge motorised fan under the seats behind the Canal End goal. The fan sucks water from the pitch and can cope with twelve inches of rain in an hour, which is far in excess of even the worst Irish conditions. The process can be reversed and the fan can blow air into the pitch to aerate the roots – if this is done when the stadium is empty you can hear the faint hiss coming up through the ground. Remarkably the first game on the pitch took place less than six months after the older one was taken up.

In 2002 the new Croke Park Stadium came of age. During the season 1.3 million people attended matches at Croke Park. As the months progressed the crowds began to move along the upper deck of the Hogan as more and more seats became ready. The first occasion on which the entirety of the Cusack, Canal and Hogan were occupied was the hurling final of 2002. Croke Park had come so far that the Nally Stand now looked shabby and Hill 16 diminutive. The teams paraded before the throw in, against a wall of noise. Any fears about the new stadium lacking in atmosphere were emphatically dispelled.

The new Croke Park had opened and the reviews were ecstatic. Photographers pored over it as if it were a fashion model. Tom Humphries of *The Irish Times* wrote:

> If you grew up in the GAA the new Croke Park is a dreamworld. Slow escalators taking people to the sky, great banks of seats making the amphitheatre and a seam of executive boxes making the money.
>
> For all the vainglorious talk down through the generations of the glory of hurling and football, the GAA never gave its jewels a showcase.

The new Croke Park is perfect. Its inviolable pitch, its softly curved roofing, its teeming terraces and its handsome bars. It is a uniquely Irish place.[3]

Vincent Hogan, of the *Irish Independent*, wrote:

For me, the beauty of the new Croke Park now is that it is truly world-class, yet remains so rich in history. Imagine moving to a greenfield site … and setting the developers loose on Croke Park? It would have been tantamount to heresy. Now the same site that housed Ring, Mackey, Doyle, Keher, O'Connell, Purcell, Heffernan, Jacko, Mullins, Spillane, Sheehy, 'Bomber', Matt Connor and the rest, still throbs to the sound of summer.

It is as it should be then. The new Croke Park honouring the old. Modern, self-confident, yet freighted with proud history. It is a union of two worlds. Each one beautifully enhanced by this fusion of stone and steel and human intellect.[4]

Simon Inglis, author and internationally recognised stadium expert, wrote of the GAA's achievement:

Here is a functional, high quality spectator facility built on sound principles. A stadium that works, does not eat up acres of green belt land, that has an established event schedule, and that has been constructed … on time and by international standards, at a very reasonable cost. I can think of a lot of cities and sporting bodies who would happily settle for that.

You'd be amazed how often those in charge of stadium redevelopments fail to achieve such ends. Even assuming they had drawn up a masterplan in the first place (which many don't), they frequently deviate from it in order to follow the latest fashion, or to upstage a predecessor (the 'my stand's bigger than yours!' syndrome). Or they may lose their nerve, or their funding, and end up with an uncomfortable compromise.[5]

Frank McDonald in *The Irish Times* wrote that Croke Park, although conceived long before the economic revival, was one of the only positive

Tommy Graham

EDITOR OF *HISTORY IRELAND* MAGAZINE

I was born in Donegal who had yet to win an Ulster title when I was born. My father came from Wicklow and my mother from Offaly and those counties had not done much either. However, the family moved to Dublin and I started to go to Croke Park from an early stage.

My first real memory is of the 1970 Leinster final between 'my team', Offaly, and Meath. It was the first year of the eighty-minute matches and it seemed very long to me but we had a big lead and I was very happy. But Meath staged one of their famous rallies with Mick Fay causing havoc as the big lead dwindled and we ended up losing.

I didn't know who to support in the 1972 All-Ireland semi-final when my native Donegal played Offaly. Although my next-door neighbour as a child in Ballyshannon, Martin Carney, was on the Donegal team but I had got used to supporting Offaly. It worked out all right in the end – Offaly won but the greatest memory I have of the game is the long-haired Martin soloing from midfield and scoring a great goal.

I was at the drawn final with Kerry that year but I recall the rain more than anything else. My brother was over from Denmark for the game and he brought a few visitors with him and they could not believe the excitement and sport attached to an All-Ireland final. I was behind the Canal goal for the famous final of 1982 when Séamus Darby scored the late goal at the other end of the field. It was raining that day too and I missed a lot of the action early on because the man in front of me had a huge umbrella up in the air and the place was too packed to move around. I solved the problem though before Martin Furlong saved the penalty right in front of us – I reached out and grabbed the umbrella and bent it in two before I handed it back to the owner.

I attended the four games between Dublin and Meath in 1991. Even though the standard of football was poor at times it was all great value. I was on the Cusack Stand for the fourth match and Hill 16 was truly in full voice coming towards the end when it looked as if the Dubs had the game won. The ending was unbelievable – Kevin Foley's equalising goal for Meath followed by David Beggy's winning point. The Hill was stunned into silence like never before.

Nowadays I organise trips to Croke Park for students from New York who come to Ireland to study.

Their first reaction is amazement at the size and excellence of the place and they find it incredible that an Association catering for amateur players could have developed it.

things to have come out of the era of the Celtic Tiger (see pages 188–189). Perhaps one of the most telling points is that the stadium has not been given a nickname by some wag. In fact its original one of 'Croker' has almost come to seem somehow disrespectful.

On 28 March 2003, 500 invited guests sat down in the conference room of the Hogan Stand for the official opening of the Canal and Hogan Stands. In attendance was a 'Who's Who' of the GAA world. After a lunch of smoked salmon, caesar salad with croutons, roast sirloin of beef with a whiskey cream sauce and chocolate and orange marquise with cointreau and almonds came the official ceremony. It began with a speech by Liam Mulvihill, who, twenty years previously, had seen the need for changes and worked more than any other person for nearly two decades to see it fulfilled. The then Taoiseach, Bertie Ahern, said 'Croke Park is a jewel of Irish life and always has, and always will be, one of my favourite places on earth.' The Lord Mayor of Dublin, Dermot Lacey said, 'Croke Park will project to the world an image of contemporary Ireland that will reflect well on Ireland, on Dublin and on Gaelic games themselves.'

After the speeches there was an ecumenical service and the blessing of the stands. The first reading was from the prophet Micah. It was chosen clearly with an eye on the impressive development;

> But in days to come
> Yahweh's Temple Mountain
> Will Tower above the mountains,
> Rise higher than the hills.
> Then people will stream to it …

The people responsible for the achievement had lived with the project for more than a decade of their lives with an intensity and commitment that can only be guessed at. Although the relationships between all involved must have been strained on occasions each would have a strong sense of pride. Project manager Chris Gogarty said it was the best thing he would do professionally. Architect Des McMahon described this time as the best days of their lives. Dermot Power said it was the best thing any of them would ever do in their lives. Liam Mulvihill has said, 'I wouldn't change anything if I were to do it all over again'.[6]

In March 2005 a redeveloped Hill 16 Terrace completed the stadium. Meanwhile a Croke Park Hotel was constructed on Jones' Road. On the completion of the Hill the capacity of Croke Park was just over 84,000 making it the third largest stadium in Europe behind the Nou Camp and Bernabeau in Spain.

The story of the construction of the stadium has been one of almost unqualified triumph. The stadium was conceived in the late 1980s. It was a time when few people were building anything in a country that had been almost in a permanent state of recession – in 1987 unemployment was 18.5 per cent and the GDP was 64 per cent of the EU average. The stadium had cost in the region of €250 million of which €70 million had been provided by the government. The final product is almost exactly the same as the drawings produced in 1992. The scale of the project was huge. The final figures for the combined new Cusack, Canal and Hogan Stands are staggering. The volume of soil excavated for the foundations was 60,000m³, 40,000m³ of granular filling was used for levelling the foundations, 2,000 concrete columns bored into the ground to a depth of 12-15m, internal wall area of the stadium was 40,000m², there were 2,000 doors, 10,000m of pipe-work, 8,000m of underground drainage, 3,000m² of external cladding and glazing, eight lifts and ten escalators. In floor area the stadium is the equivalent of a building with a floor area of nearly 1 million square feet. In addition to this the roof area is 200,000 square feet. The length of the stepped terracing is 26 miles, i.e., if you were to start at the first row at one end of the Cusack Stand and run to the end of the Hogan then move up to the next row and so on until you reached the last row of the top of the upper deck you would have run the equivalent of a marathon.[7]

Originally it was thought that the redevelopment would take fifteen years. It was finished ahead of schedule. During this period a full schedule of games was held during the whole of the construction – a reflection of very tight planning. In a country where any major project seems to be ill-planned, poorly costed, behind schedule and disappointing when it is completed, the reconstruction of Croke Park represents an almost unique achievement in modern Ireland.

Throughout its history Croke Park had always been a reflection of the GAA and an influence on it. According to its executive architect, Des McMahon, 'the stadium defines the Gaelic Athletic Association's aspirations in dramatic terms'.[8] Now the stadium had become almost a symbol of a new vibrant Ireland. Ironically, bringing the new Croke Park

Women's Football supporters at Croke Park.

to a reality embroiled the stadium in one of the most controversial episodes in the history.

OPENING CROKE PARK

There are few countries in the world where the issues around its stadiums could cause controversy on a scale seen in Ireland in the late twentieth and early twenty-first centuries.

The root cause of the controversy was that the other main stadium in Ireland at Lansdowne Road, the international home of the Irish Rugby Football Union and the Football Association of Ireland, had long ceased to fulfil the requirements of either modern sporting organisations or their followers. With the success of the Irish national soccer team in the 1990 World Cup the government made tentative moves towards building a national stadium. For a time the GAA (already advancing its own plans)

Paul Reilly

AN EYEWITNESS TO BLOODY SUNDAY, CROKE PARK, 1920

I was born in 1910 and lived on the North Circular Road. I was ten years old when I witnessed the attack at Croke Park on Bloody Sunday. I was a volunteer at Croke Park and the day before the match between Tipperary and Dublin we spent most of the day cutting the grass and marking the pitch. On the day of Bloody Sunday I arrived at about 11.00 to put down the flags and put the nets up in the goals. I then worked at one of the entrance stiles.

There was no sense of any danger that day. As far as I can remember I had no knowledge of the killing of the spies that morning. We did not learn about it until the next day. Anyway, it wasn't news that there had been shootings in Dublin. It seemed like it would be a normal match day.

Just as the match had started British soldiers came through the gate at the railway end and began to search people for arms. About twenty minutes later the Black and Tans arrived at the Canal End gate. This was not an entrance gate but a hedge and small gate for officials to enter. For some reason or another they started firing on the crowd especially in the direction of the people on Hill 16 and those on the pitch. There was huge confusion and the crowd trampled quite a number of people. There were only four St John's Ambulancemen on duty. The injured were taken to the Mater Hospital by sidecar and cabs which would normally have taken people back to the railway stations after the match.

The firing lasted no more than three or four minutes. When it finished the Black and Tans came into the ground and started searching people. Two lorries of spectators were taken away. The Tans took up the flags from the pitch as souvenirs. They seemed intent to continue the shooting. The senior army officer went to the senior officer of the Black and Tans and argued with him for fifteen minutes to stop the shooting. At this point the British soldiers helped to tend the injured. Although everyone afterwards blames the soldiers as well as the Black and Tans, it was just the Black and Tans who did the shooting.

considered the options presented by the government move. These included relocating to a joint national stadium on a greenfield site or making its own ground at Jones' Road the national stadium. Of course in the end the GAA went its own way. For the next decade schemes for other stadiums appeared and disappeared with some regularity – among the proposed sites were Neilstown and the Phoenix Park. One of the more serious proposals came in 1998 when the Football Association of Ireland declared its intention to break away from Lansdowne Road and build its own stadium at an estimated cost of £65 million. The site chosen was adjacent to the City West Campus. Naming rights were negotiated with Eircom and the project became known as 'Eircom Park'.

Meanwhile the government, led by the Taoiseach Bertie Ahern, resurrected the idea of a national stadium. In 2000 it launched its plan to construct an 80,000-seat stadium in Abbotstown, west Dublin, to be called 'Stadium Ireland'. After a short but tortuous history, the Eircom Park project was shelved in March 2001 when the FAI decided to row in with the government's idea for a national stadium. Helping to pave the way for this decision was a government promise to the FAI of £45 million over three years.

At the GAA's Annual Congress in 2000 in Galway, former President of the GAA Peter Quinn raised the prospect of Croke Park being opened to other games. He made reference to merely financial considerations. The Croke Park budget had been hit by the construction cost inflation caused by the Celtic Tiger (wages in the construction industry alone increased by 50 per cent in three years). Quinn said that in his opinion they had a number of options: 'We can pay £5 million a year for ten years. We can ask the government for a £50 million grant. We can consider leasing Croke Park or we could become the national stadium. I believe we should talk to the government and see if they are interested in doing business.'[9]

The stadium certainly represented a huge financial investment for the GAA. In the end it would cost in the region of €250 million. However, there was also the question of ongoing running and maintenance costs estimated to be in the region of €3-4 million per annum. Such was the task involved in running the stadium, a separate management company, Páirc an Chrocaigh Teoranta under Peter McKenna and reporting to a Stadium Executive, was set up for Croke Park. Amongst the membership of the Association there were fears that these costs could be passed down to the

An aerial view of Croke Park with the Hogan Stand in the foreground.

clubs throughout the country in a 'Croke Park levy'. For many it made little sense that such a fantastic facility that cost so much should have no sporting events between the All-Ireland football final at the end of September (or the International Rules series in October) and the club finals on St Patrick's day, with the Croke Park season proper not starting until June.

In December 2000 the annual convention of the Kilkenny county board voted 31-5 in favour of the opening of Croke Park on financial grounds. It was the beginning of a move that would ultimately see motion number six on the agenda for the GAA's Annual Congress held in the Burlington Hotel on 7 April 2001 address the issue of opening Croke Park. The motion was proposed by Tommy Kenoy of the Kilmore Club in Roscommon. It read 'Central Council shall have the power to authorise the use of Croke Park in certain circumstances for field games other than those controlled by the association' (another motion from Longford calling for the opening of all GAA grounds was abandoned as it had little chance of success). The Roscommon motion sought to amend Rule 42 (b) of the GAA rule book which stated that 'grounds controlled by association units shall not be used, or permitted to be used, for horse racing, greyhound racing or for field games other than those sanctioned by the Central Council'. On the face of it 42 (b) did not rule out other games, but reference was made elsewhere in the rules to 'purposes not in conflict with the association' and it was understood that for something as dramatic as opening Croke Park to competing sports a change of the rule was required.

Apart from finance there were other considerations. Croke Park was now something that members of the association were immensely proud of and many were warming to the idea that it was something to be shown off to others. Bringing other people into Croke Park could only enhance the standing of Gaelic games. The sweeping stands at Jones' Road were a reflection of a proud and vibrant association that should have no fear to allow other people to use its facilities and to have them pay handsomely for that privilege.

A whole host of concerns were expressed in the press, in bars, kitchens, club houses, dressing rooms and meetings. If the GAA did not open up they might lose out on future funding. It was also felt that they should open while the going was good – once the national stadium was completed the financial boat would have left. Against these considerations was tradition and fear of undermining local clubs. The association was built on tradition,

Supporters going into Croke Park.

A view of Croke Park.

Brian O'Driscoll

FORMER CAPTAIN OF THE IRISH RUGBY TEAM

I had never played in Croke Park but loved to go to games, especially when the Dubs were playing. Thanks to Sean Kelly and the GAA, rugby came to 'Croker' and having missed the French game through injury, I could hardly wait to get out on the pitch for the match against England. I know that in the past over 90,000 had attended games in Croke Park but the thought of even 84,000 passionate supporters watching a rugby match at GAA headquarters excited me greatly. Lansdowne Road has served rugby well but urgently needed redevelopment. To have Croke Park as a temporary home was an unbelievable bonus. It has everything: a state of the art stadium, headquarters of the GAA with its memorable history and a chance for twice the number of spectators to watch and support Ireland playing rugby at home. At times I thought it surreal.

On taking the field I was immediately struck by the massive 'green' replacing the normal inter-county colours and will never forget the roar of the crowd welcoming us. Listening to the national anthems was both spine tingling and emotional. Our victory seemed to create a national euphoria and truly one of the great days for Irish rugby will always be associated with Croke Park.

with Croke Park as the GAA's heartland and home. Croke Park had become synonymous with the GAA. It was not the GAA's fault that as an amateur organisation it had succeeded in the realisation of its fantastical vision. If the other, professional, organisations could not get their house in order it was not the business of the GAA to bail them out. In addition it was also feared that opening Croke Park might also lead to pressure on its other grounds. As one person put it, 'There are villages in the country where the facilities are the only advantage Gaelic games have. Soccer is wall-to-wall on the television but the GAA have the dressing rooms, the bar, the covered seating. Take away those and share them out to other sports and of course the games would suffer.'[10]

Those brave enough to predict the outcome of the vote at Congress thought it would fall just short. There were a number of structural factors working against a change; according to the rules of Congress a two-thirds majority was needed to make a rule change and those who attended Congress were older and more conservative than the main body of the association; neither President McCague nor the GAA management felt it appropriate to provide direction to the delegates on how they should vote on such an important issue.

Tom Humphries wrote an emotional plea in *The Irish Times* the week before the congress: 'Once, just once, couldn't the organisation stand up straight, do itself a favour, and make a grand gesture? Please.'[11] One thing was certain on the Friday afternoon; this was going to be a momentous decision either way. With a dramatic scene already set, a bolt came from the blue. The night before the Congress the Taoiseach announced that a grant of £60 million would be made available to the GAA to assist in the completion of the stadium in time to host the opening of the Special Olympics (only half of which was eventually forthcoming). Suddenly the financial argument that had underpinned the proposed change of rule vanished. The overdraft on Croke Park would drop to just £25 million and the stadium debt would be gone in a few years. While people were still floundering under the impact of the announcement, the vote was held on Saturday afternoon.

With a two-thirds majority needed, the motion was defeated by one vote – 176 for, 89 against and 44 abstentions. Despite the importance of the issue the vote was totted with a head count of the delegates. Calls for a recount were rejected.

All hell broke loose.

The newspaper headlines were scathing – 'Jaded Minority Holding Progress to Ransom', 'Dinosaurs, Last Stand', 'Democracy at its Worst'. The Taoiseach was accused of intentionally undermining the yes vote to keep Croke Park closed, thus keeping his Stadium Ireland ambitions on track. Paradoxically the GAA was attacked for not voting for the opening up of Croke Park after having just been given substantial funds out of the public coffers. The Taoiseach was urged by his partners in government, the Progressive Democrats, and opposition parties to insist that the grant be conditional on Croke Park being opened. He replied that he had no power to compel the GAA to change its rule. Critics of the GAA called the vote narrow-minded and bigoted – for many Croke Park was just too good for the GAA to selfishly keep to themselves. Meanwhile, those who voted

against the proposal came under scrutiny; some counties' delegates had not previously consulted their clubs as to how they should vote; some ignored instructions; some delegations changed their minds after the Taoiseach's announcement. For weeks Croke Park was national headline news in a way that it had not been since Bloody Sunday in 1920.

In the immediate aftermath of the vote, those who supported the motion took comfort from the fact that the vote was so close. It seemed inevitable that the 2002 Annual Congress would provide the necessary two-thirds majority. However, when Rule 42 was voted on for the second time it was resoundingly defeated. This reversal was put down to the backlash against the GAA in the aftermath of the previous vote; if the GAA was going to open Croke Park it was going to do so when it wanted to, not when others wanted.

The story was, of course, not dead yet. The government put forward Croke Park as one of the venues for the joint Irish-Scottish bid for the 2008 European Soccer Championships on the understanding that a vote at Congress was still needed. When the delegation of UEFA officials came to Dublin to view the proposed venues they went to Lansdowne Road, which was clearly not up to scratch, they went to the proposed site of the national stadium at Abbotstown to look at a field for which funding had been refused the week before, and they visited Croke Park which, according to the rules of the GAA, could not host soccer games. Such a situation cannot have helped the failed bid.

The latest twists in the saga came in 2004 when the government finally gave approval to the construction of a national stadium to be built on the site of Lansdowne Road. In the spring of 2004 all motions relating to the opening of Croke Park put forward for the GAA's Annual Congress were ruled out of order. It was always unlikely to be the end of the story.

COLISEUM

Meanwhile, away from the controversy, the stadium delighted those who went to Croke Park for matches.

Facing page: Croke Park hosts the opening ceremony of the 2003 Special Olympics. Here, the first teams parade into the stadium.

Despite the heroics that the arena has witnessed one of the most important occasions was the opening ceremony of the 2003 Special Olympics held in Croke Park. It was the first time the event was held outside the United States. Nearly ninety years after it hosted the *Tailteann* Games, Croke Park was once again the only venue in Ireland that could cope with such an event. The night featured Nelson Mandela, Muhammed Ali (one reporter asked if Ali had 'wondered if this really was the same place he fought Al Blue Lewis three decades ago?'), U2, The Corrs, Roy Keane, Ronnie Delany, Brian Kerr, D.J. Carey, An Taoiseach Bertie Ahern, President Mary McAleese among many others. The most important guests, of course, were the 11,000 athletes competing at the games. During the first part of the evening, the teams from every nation in the world paraded into GAA headquarters. The first team into Croke Park was Greece, led out by Sean Kelly, GAA President.

Going beyond mere sport, the evening embraced a way to view the world with Croke Park as the spectacular backdrop. When the Irish team entered the arena 80,000 people began to chant 'Ole Ole Ole' and those who knew the stadium knew this was something special, something never seen before. Of all the performers only Bono of U2 perhaps sensed the moment when he rooted the event in Croke Park during his introduction to Nelson Mandela – 'Croke Park, June 21, Croke Park, June 21 …'

In its more traditional role the new stadium excelled. Average attendances increased by between 5-10,000 per match at Croke Park. Prior to the redevelopment Croke Park would generally be sold out for two or three games a year. In 2003 there were eight full houses. As well as encouraging supporters to go to more games, those who had never thought of going to GAA headquarters found themselves at the home of Gaelic games. Architect Des McMahon remembers overhearing well-to-do women in a south Dublin pub boasting of how many times they had been to Croke Park that year. The term 'Croke Park chic' was used to describe the phenomenon. Unbelievably, Croke Park had become trendy. In April 2002 guided tours of the stadium organised by the GAA Museum were packed out every day.

On the pitch, tradition and innovation were in evidence in equal measure. It seemed to be a perfect reflection of the stadium and its connection to its rich past.

In 2002 Kilkenny faced Clare in the hurling All-Ireland. The Kilkenny Cats gave a virtuoso display. D.J. Carey left an indelible memory on the minds of the 79,500 spectators. His third-minute goal set the scene for the day. Then, in the fifty-fourth minute, he caught the ball in midfield and went on a solo run. With the sliotar on the boss of his hurley, he twisted and turned with two Claremen in pursuit. He lost one, then jinked, twisted and turned until the unfortunate Ollie Baker fell in a tangle of legs and arms. D.J. then rolled the ball still on the end of his hurley and sent it between the posts. It was a classic moment from the greatest hurler of the modern era. In the next year, Kilkenny once again asserted their dominance when they defeated Cork.

In contrast to the hurling, the first football All-Ireland finals played in the near-completed Croke Park resulted in two counties winning the title for the first time. In 2002 Armagh, who had never won an All-Ireland, faced the traditional power of Kerry. It was Armagh's third attempt while Kerry had won more All-Irelands than any other county. At half-time Kerry had outplayed the men in orange but were still only four points clear. Like the 1953 final, Armagh failed to convert a penalty. However, in the second half Armagh – inspired by Joe Kiernan's half-time dressing room dismissal of his 1977 losers medal – smothered a panicked Kerry and won by a point. After the final whistle the pitch became a sea of orange – any idea of preventing a pitch invasion was abandoned.

In 2003 the 'back door' system saw the first ever all-Ulster final between Tyrone and defending champions Armagh. None could recall the National Anthem being sung with such respect. The match was tense and close but Peter Canavan's Tyrone went on to lift the Sam Maguire for the first time in their history. The pitch became a sea of Tyrone red and white.

Soon after the 2003 season came to an end the fourth and final phase of the modernisation of Croke Park began with the demolition of Hill 16. In a sense things had come full circle. It was out of the reconstruction of Hill 16 in the 1980s that the idea of rebuilding the entire stadium had arisen. Now, fifteen years later, the terracing was demolished again to make way for the final element of the project. To their eternal credit the GAA won the fight to retain the Hill as a terrace. In late 2004 Hill 16 was opened.

On 16 April 2005 in what had obviously been a hard, tortuous and soul-searching decision for the GAA, a motion giving Central Council power to permit the use of Croke Park during the redevelopment of

Lansdowne Road was passed by a vote of 227 to 97. The prospect of Irish sporting teams having to play 'home' games in Britain, outgoing President Sean Kelly's consistent support for the opening of Croke Park, the decision to have a secret ballot and perhaps a change of guard in the GAA ranks all played a part in the decision.

Before the first rugby and soccer matches were played a number of changes took place. In September 2005 the Croke Park Hotel (run by Jurys) opened on Jones' Road. The hotel became another pillar in the commercial success of the stadium. In April 2006 various parts of the stadium were named after some of the association's historic figures – the Canal End became the (Maurice) Davin Stand, Frank Dineen, who bought the ground and later sold it to the GAA, was commemorated with the renaming of Hill 16 to Dineen/Hill 16. Luke O'Toole, Pádraig Ó Caoimh and Seán Ó Síocháin were also commemorated with the naming of internal sections of the stadium, while broadcaster Mícheál Ó Hehir had the press area named in his honour. On 3 February 2007 the final touches were put to nearly twenty years of Croke Park's redevelopment when a state of the art set of floodlights were first switched on for the first round National League football match between Tyrone and Dublin. A full house of 82,000 witnessed the event. It was the best attended sporting event in the world that weekend.

The first rugby match played at Croke Park was against France on 11 February 2007. In the run up to the match Croke Park once again dominated all talk and media headlines. In the stadium everything was being prepared, from the unfamiliar sight of rugby goalposts and markings to a member of staff going around corporate level with a brush and buckets of white paint, touching up any areas that had been marked – the GAA was putting its best silver on display and no one was going to have anything to complain about.

At the top of Jones' Road people forlornly held the traditional makeshift signs aloft looking for tickets. There was not a ticket in sight. Scores of coaches made their way northside from the rugby strongholds near Lansdowne Road. A television helicopter followed the Irish team bus as it crossed the city. Paul O'Connell, Irish captain, led out his team onto the hallowed turf. No north and south terrace here, or East and West stand, but a stadium freighted with history: Michael Hogan's stand, Michael Cusack's stand, Pat Nally's terrace, the Davin stand, Hill 16.

The occasion was charged with significance but the atmosphere was curious. There was no banter typical of a GAA match featuring two rival counties. There was little sway of emotion or noise between two equal groups of supporters as is customary at headquarters. It was something not seen in Croke Park before. A competitive game but the vast majority were supporters of the one team: no roughly evenly spread supporters in a Kerry-Tyrone crowd, or Dublin-Armagh or Kilkenny-Cork. Long periods of the game were played in a French-inspired near silence. But when Ronan O'Gara scored the first Irish try at Croke Park there had never been as unified a roar in the stadium's history. In the end Ireland lost a thrilling match 20-17 to a last-minute French try: another Croke Park first, a unified silence of the vast majority of a defeated crowd. Croke Park had always been about celebration in the end someone won – but on this occasion Ireland and the vast majority of its supporters lost.

After all the arguments and debate about the opening of Croke Park, the playing of the French game did not end the controversy. On Saturday 24 February the English rugby team were to play in Croke Park and the issue of the playing of 'God Save the Queen' came centre stage. That the anthem would be played in the ground where fourteen innocent civilians were killed on Bloody Sunday 1920 raised the emotional level for some. When it finally came, the playing of 'God Save the Queen' for the first time at Croke Park was a momentous occasion that transcended sport. A pregnant silence preceded the anthem. It was warmly applauded at its close. Rarely was an anthem so respected. When it came to the singing of 'Amhrán na bhFiann' seasoned and hard rugby men like John Hayes and Jerry Flannery were overcome with emotion on the pitch. They were not alone. It was an incredible few minutes. Such moments are seldom in life. At the end of eighty minutes' play Ireland had produced a stunning performance, beating England by a record margin (a curious footnote was that Ireland's first try was scored by Girvan Dempsey, remarkably close to the spot where Michael Hogan had been killed in 1920). In the end the scoreboard read Ireland 43 England 13. A match was over and, in many ways, a Rubicon had been crossed.

A collective sigh of relief was nearly audible when, on 22 March, the go ahead was given by the planning board for the redevelopment of Lansdowne Road. The joint venture between the IRFU and the FAI is estimated to cost €41 million of which the government supplied in excess of €191 million – over three times the level of government support for Croke Park. With the announcement, any question of Croke Park having to permanently accommodate other sports was safely put to bed. However, given the positive experiences it is likely that even though the southside stadium is fully operational, there may be future rugby and soccer games at Croke Park on an intermittent basis.

The first soccer match at Croke Park was anticlimactic in comparison to the rugby. On Saturday 24 March 2007 Ireland beat Wales 1-0 (the first soccer goal was scored by Stephen Ireland). Rarely was a more tepid match played at Croke Park. According to *The Irish Times* soccer correspondent Emmet Malone 'those GAA delegates who opposed "soccer" being allowed into Croke Park for fear that international games played on the country's greatest sporting stage would further boost the growth of the association's chief rival for young hearts and minds must have slept a little easier on Saturday night'. The following Wednesday a vibrant display against Slovakia restored some sense of occasion.

Just two months later the championship got into full swing as Croke Park went back to what it had always done best, being the focus of the Gaelic games world.

Within a short period of time the extraordinary became ordinary as rugby and soccer matches came and went each year with little further comment on the significance of the change that had been undertaken. While the futuristic Aviva Stadium rose into the air on the south side of the city, income generated from facilitating the matches tumbled into GAA accounts. During the four years in which the Irish soccer team played thirteen matches and the rugby team twelve (plus one Heineken Cup semi-final) at Croke Park, over €35 million was generated for the Association. Even in a boom economy this was a tidy sum. However, by the time the Aviva was opened the economic landscape in Ireland had changed utterly.

When the Celtic Tiger economy collapsed it was curious how Croke Park, a sports stadium, became part of the national discussion as the country tried to make sense of its recent past and to chart a way forward.

Firstly, amidst the onset of the deepest of recessions, people looked around to see what the country had to show for all the apparent wealth it had so recently had. To some leading commentators the rebuilt Croke Park was one of the few positive legacies of the Celtic Tiger. However, such assessments, though well intentioned, were fundamentally mistaken.

Because Croke Park was not a legacy of the boom years. Indeed, quite the opposite is true. Croke Park was conceived in the mid- to late 1980s, at the depth of the last recession, and its construction began in the autumn of 1993, well before the first roars of the new Tiger economy. Perhaps the lesson to be drawn from the redevelopment of Croke Park is that, even in dire economic circumstances, if one has courage, vision and commitment great things can still be achieved.

Another curious role that Croke Park played in the new circumstances came from an unusual event held at Croke Park. In June 2010 the stadium was the venue for negotiations between the government and the public service unions to thrash out a reform deal to help see the country through the crisis. The deal, which established the public sector agenda for the coming years, was officially known as the Public Service Agreement 2010–2014, but it almost universally became known as known as the 'Croke Park Agreement' or, simply, 'Croke Park'.

The post-Celtic Tiger era has presented the GAA with serious challenges. Emigration once again blights a generation. Clubs are losing members. Advertising and television revenue are down. And there has been an impact in the stands. The days of regular sell outs – or near sell outs – at Croke Park are now in the past. While the novelty of attending matches in the 'new' Croke Park has worn off people also simply do not have spare money in their pockets. New ticket packages and reductions in prices have alleviated the potential impact but there may still be some way to go as austerity is set to continue.

Meanwhile, the completed Aviva has not only removed the welcome extra income from matches at Croke Park once banned under Rule 42, it has also become a competitor in the market for sponsorship, corporate events, long term ticket sales and concerts. But the Aviva will always be a smaller venue than Croke Park and one that could never have held three U2 concerts (24, 25 and 27 July 2009) with nearly a quarter of a million people in attendance. However, there is another more prosaic reason that the Aviva Stadium on Lansdowne Road will never compete with Croke Park on Jones' Road. That is historical resonance.

In March 2011 the historical importance of Croke Park once again took centre stage when it was announced that Queen Elizabeth II of England was to visit Ireland. The first visit by a British head of state in a century was going to be a confrontation with history. The one event that caught the imagination of the Irish and British public was a scheduled visit to Croke Park. It was a brave and bold decision and one born from President McAleese's great interest in the GAA as well as the symbolism of that night in February 2007 when 'God Save the Queen' was played at the stadium.

The Queen's visit turned out to be even more significant than anyone had thought possible. It changed the relationship between Britain and Ireland forever.

Just after 3pm on 18 May, the second day of her four-day visit, the Queen arrived at Croke Park. By that stage she had already been to the Garden of Remembrance and the War Memorial Gardens and perhaps it was for that reason that the stadium visit was not a solemn one weighted down with politics but one that had more of the atmosphere of a visit to Ireland's largest sporting and cultural association.

Though the visit did not lack symbolism on a number of levels – at the entrance children waving the flags of the thirty-two counties (plus New York and London) was a reminder that the GAA was an all-Ireland organisation – and Christy Cooney made specific reference to those killed at Croke Park, the time the Queen spent at Croke Park was remarkably relaxed.

When the Queen, accompanied by President McAleese and GAA President Christy Cooney, walked down the tunnel and into an icon of Irish nationalism the stadium was without its essential ingredients of players and spectators. Due to understandable security concerns the only presence was the Artane Band and scores of the world's photojournalists in a designated area capturing the historic moment. The group, made up of the Queen, Prince Philip, President McAleese and her husband Martin, Christy Cooney and Ard Stiúrthóir, Padraig Duffy, chatted amiably and the scene was friendly, genial and, in a curious way, almost normal. The images belied the drama of the text of the Sky News alert, 'The Queen Visiting Croke Park to Pay Tribute to Victims of Massacre'. After forty-five minutes the Queen of England left and another historic event at Croke Park was over.

On 6 June 2012 history returned once again to the stadium as the first leg of the Dublin Olympic torch relay took place at Croke Park – the bearer was the great Kilkenny hurler, Henry Shefflin. But this leg did not take place on the pitch or even in the stands. It took place on new Etihad Skyline walkway that was built at a cost of €1m on top of the stands. The

Skyline opened for business on 1 June and offers unrivalled views over the capital city while also including a terrifying section that juts out above eleven storeys of empty space. It is just another of the revenue streams created by Stadium Director Peter McKenna (now also Commercial Director of the GAA) to help Croke Park to generate income for the GAA. But still the events on the pitch retain their central importance in the story of the stadium with Tipperary's denial of Kilkenny's hurling five-in-a-row and Dublin's last point victory over Kerry in the 2011 All-Ireland final just two of the games that will live long in the memory of the stadium.

On 22 December 2013 Croke Park will be a hundred years old. One hundred years since the City and Suburban Sports Ground was purchased by the GAA. What had been bought simply as a sporting venue has, over time, become not only an expression of the GAA, but an Irish icon. The centenary of Croke Park is one that is defined by matches, by events and, at its heart, by the stories of the millions of people who have passed through its turnstiles (or been lifted over them), who were left changed by what they saw on the pitch enclosed by stands loaded with history.

References

CHAPTER ONE

1   O'Hehir, Brendan, *Over the Bar: a personal relationship with the GAA*, Ward River Press, Dublin, 1984, p. 215-6.

2   *Gaelic News*, July 1897.

3   De Búrca, Marcus, *The GAA: A History*, Gill & Macmillan, 1999, p. 38.

4   Vaughan, Joseph D., *Liffey Gaels, A Century of Gaelic Games, 1884-1984*, Liffey Gaels, Dublin, 1984, p. 107.

5   Horgan, Tim, *Cork's Hurling Story, From 1890 to the Present Time*, Anvil Books, Dublin, 1977, p. 9.

6   Foley, Patrick, Kerry's Football Story, *The Kerryman*, Tralee 1945, p. 26.

7   Horgan, op. cit., p. 15.

8   Ibid., p. 21.

9   GAA, 1915 Yearbook, *The Gaelic Press,* Dublin, 1915, p. 42.

10 *The Irish Daily Independent*, 23 March 1896.

11 *Sport*, 28 March 1896.

12 De Búrca, op. cit., p. 66.

13 O'Ceallaigh, Seamus, *Gaelic Days*, Gaelic Athletic Publications, Limerick, 1944, p. 78.

14 *An Caman*, Iul 1931.

15 *Sport*, 10 June 1904.

16 *Irish Independent*, GAA Golden Jubilee Number, Easter 1934, p. 15.

17 *Sport*, 8 August 1903.

18 Foley, op. cit., p 21.

19 Corry, Eoghan, Kildare GAA, *A Centenary History*, Kildare County Board, Newbridge, 1984, p. 60.

20 *Sport*, 30 July 1904.

21 *Sport*, 22 October 1904.

22 *Sport*, 19 November 1904.

23 *Sport*, 4 February 1905.

24   *Sport* , 21 April 1906.

25   *Sport,* 28 October 1905.

26   De Búrca, op. cit., p. 68 and p. 75.

27   *Sport,* 23 October 1909.

28   *Sport,* 1 May 1909.

29   *Sport,* 11 December 1909.

30   *Sport,* 8 February 1913.

31   *Sport,* 29 March 1913.

32   *Sport,* 3 May 1913.

33   *Sport,* 10 May 1913.

34   *Sport,* 14 June 1913.

35   *Sport,* 21 June 1913.

36   *Sport,* 24 May 1913.

37   *Sport,* 1 July 1913.

38   *Sport,* 5 July 1913.

39   De Búrca, op. cit., pp. 90-91.

40   *Sport,* 4 December 1913.

CHAPTER TWO

1   *The Irish Times,* 2 September 1995.

2   *Irish Independent,* GAA Golden Jubliee Number, Easter, 1934, p. 22.

3   *Sport,* 3 December 1914.

4   *Sport,* 24 October 1914.

5   *Sport,* 3 April 1915.

6   *Sport,* 29 March 1919.

7   De Búrca, op. cit., p. 118.

8   Handbill, ILB 300 p3, National Library of Ireland.

9   *Freeman's Journal,* 7 April 1919.

10   *Sport,* 30 October 1919.

11   *Sport,* 6 November 1920.

12   O'Meára, Micheál (Ed), *Bloody Sunday; 1920-1995,* Tipperary County
      Board, Thurles, 1995, pp.14-16.

13 Gleeson, James, *Bloody Sunday*, Four Square, London, 1963, p. 138.

14 *Freeman's Journal*, 24 November 1920.

15 Gleeson, op. cit., p. 139.

16 British Military inquiry into Shootings at Croke Park, 21 November 1920, War Officer Files (WO) 35/88, Public Records Office, Kew, London, England.

17 Ed. Micheál O'Meára, op. cit., p. 20.

18 Gleeson, op. cit., p. 137.

19 British military inquiry, op. cit.

20 *Irish Independent*, 23 November 1920.

21 British Military inquiry, op. cit.

22 *Irish Independent*, 23 November 1920.

23 *Freeman's Journal*, 26 November 1920.

24 *Sport*, 16 July 1921.

25 *Freeman's Journal*, 23 February 1922.

26 *Freeman's Journal*, 24 February 1922.

27 *Freeman's Journal*, 27 February 1922.

28 *Freeman's Journal*, 6 May 1922.

29 *Irish Independent*, 12 June 1922.

30 *Freeman's Journal*, 10 October 1922.

31 *Freeman's Journal*, 21 February 1923.

32 *Freeman's Journal*, 8 May 1923.

33 *Freeman's Journal*, 4 June 1923.

34 *Freeman's Journal*, 5 June 1923.

35 *Freeman's Journal*, 17 July 1922.

36 *Freeman's Journal*, 17 January 1924.

37 Mandle, W.F., *The GAA and Irish Nationalist Politics, 1884-1924*, Christopher Helm, London, 1987, p. 215.

38 *Irish Independent*, 4 August 1924.

39 *Freeman's Journal*, 19 August 1924.

40 *Freeman's Journal*, 22 August 1924.

41 *Freeman's Journal*, 19 August 1924.

CHAPTER THREE

1   O'Ceallaigh, Seamus, *Story of the GAA*, Wellbrook Press, Freshford, 1977, p. 113.

2   *Irish Independent*, GAA Golden Jubilee Number, Easter, 1934.

3   The GAA Annual, 1945, p. 19.

4   *Irish Independent*, GAA Golden Jubilee Number, Easter, 1934, p. 50.

5   The GAA Annual, 1945, p. 17 and p. 18.

6   *Irish Independent*, 7 September 1925.

7   *Irish Independent*, 18 October 1926.

8   *Irish Independent*, 13 April 1925.

9   Clarke, Paddy, *Dublin Calling*, RTE, Dublin, 1986, p. 56.

10   Kilfeather, Sean, *Vintage Carbery*, Beaver Row Press, Dublin 1984, p. 32.

11   Irish Radio Journal, 11 September 1926, Volume 2, No. 63, p. 1993.

12   *Irish Independent*, 6 September 1926.

13   *An Caman*, September 1931.

14   O'Ceallaigh, Seamus, *Gaelic Athletic Memories*, Gaelic Athletic Publications, Limerick, 1945, p. 69.

15   O'Ceallaigh (1944), op. cit., p. 27.

16   Ibid., p. 129.

17   Ibid., p. 75-77.

18   Ibid., p. 75.

19   Kilfeather, op. cit., p. 47.

20   See Match programme, 21 August 1938.

21   *Irish Press*, 22 August 1938.

22   *Irish Press*, 27 September 1943.

23   Mahon, Jack, *A History of Gaelic Football*, Gill & Macmillan, Dublin, 2000, p 73.

24   *Irish Press*, 27 September 1943.

25   *Irish Press*, 28 September 1943.

26   *Irish Press*, 11 October 1943.

27   D. 83222, I Did Penal Serviture, Metropolitan Publishing, Dublin, 1945, p. 162.

28   The GAA Annual, 1944, p. 41.

29   *Roscomáin: the Champions*, The Park Side Press, Dublin, 1945, p. 6.

CHAPTER FOUR

1   *Irish Press*, 4 September 1947.

2   King, Seamus J., A History of Hurling, Gill & Macmillan, Dublin 1998, p. 112.

3   Cumann Luthcleas Gael, Offical Records, 1951, p. 62.

4   1948 Football Final Programme.

5   *Irish Press*, 27 September 1948.

6   De Búrca, op. cit., p. 180.

7   Capuchin Annual, 1965, Symposium of Tributes to the Late Pádraig Ó Caoimh, p. 303.

8   Puirseal, Padraig, A Tribute to Padraig Ó Caoimh, Cuchulainn, Annual, 1964, pp. 59 & 66.

9   Ibid., p. 305.

10 *Irish Press*, 28 October 1949.

11 *Irish Press*, 25 September 1953.

12 GAA Digest, Annual Edition, 1950, p. 6.

13 *Irish Press*, 27 September 1952.

14 *Irish Press*, 29 September 1953.

15 Hurling Final Programme, 1953.

16 *Irish Press*, 15 June 1959.

17 *Irish Press*, 13 April 1966.

18 *Irish Independent*, 13 April 1966.

19 *Irish Press*, 6 September 1954.

20 Hurling Final Programme, September 4, 1955.

21 *Irish Press*, 26 September 1955.

22 Football Final Programme, 1952, p. 19.

23 Football Final Programme, 1956, p. 17.

24 Fullam, Brendan, *Off the Field and On: Triumphs and Trials of Gaelic Games*, Wolfhound, Dublin 1999, p. 79.

25 Our Games 1960, p. 120-121.

26 *Irish Press*, 8 June 1959.

27 *Irish Independent*, 25 September 1961.

28 *Irish Independent*, 2 September 1966.

29 Report of the Commission on the GAA, CLG, Dublin, 1 December 1971, p. 77.

30   *Irish Press*, 27 September 1965.

31   *Irish Independent*, 2 September 1963.

32   *Irish Independent*, 2 September 1963.

33   Commemorative booklet for the opening of the redeveloped Canal End
     and Hogan Stands, 28th March, GAA, 2003, p.31.

34   Report of the Commission on the GAA, op. cit., p. 47.

35   Ibid., p 48.

CHAPTER FIVE

1   Blát, booklet commemorating the opening of the Hogan Stand, GAA,
     Dublin, 1959, p. 4.

2   Croke Park Masterplan.

3   *Irish Times Magazine*, 7 September 2002.

4   Commemorative booklet (2003), op. cit., p. 31.

5   Ibid., p. 39.

6   Ibid., p. 67.

7   For a detailed study of the engineering aspect of Croke Park see Murray, F.V.,
     'Croke Park redevelopment – stadium design in an urban context', in
     Proceedings of the Institution of Civil Engineers, Structures and Buildings, 2000,
     140, November, p. 345-53.

8   Programme of the opening of the redeveloped Canal End and Hogan Stands,
     28 March 2003, p. 67.

9   *The Irish Times*, 19 April 2000.

10   *The Irish Times*, 22 November 2000.

11   *The Irish Times*, 2 April 2001.

Bibliography

NEWSPAPERS

Freeman's Journal
Irish Independent
Irish Press
Sport
The Irish Times

PERIODICALS

An Caman
Capuchin Annual
Cuchulann Annual
GAA Digest
Gaelic News
Irish Radio Journal
Our Games Annual
Proceedings of the Institution of Civil Engineers
Stadia
The GAA Annual

BOOKS

Clarke, Paddy, *Dublin Calling*, RTE, Dublin, 1986.

Corry, Eoghan, Kildare GAA, *A Centenary History*, Kildare County Board, Newbridge, 1984.

D. 83222, *I Did Penal Servitude*, Metropolitan Publishing, Dublin, 1945.

De Búrca, Marcus, *The GAA: A History*, Gill & Macmillan, Dublin, 1999.

Foley, Patrick, *Kerry's Football Story*, The Kerryman, Tralee, 1945.

Fullam, Brendan, *Off the Field and On: Triumphs and Trials of Gaelic Games*, Wolfhound Press, Dublin, 1999.

Gaelic Athletic Association, Commemorative Booklet for the opening of the Canal End and Hogan Stands, 28 March 2003, GAA, Dublin, 2003.

Gleeson, James, *Bloody Sunday*, Four Square, London, 1963.

Horgan, Tim, *Cork's Hurling Story, From 1890 to the Present Time*, Anvil Books, Dublin, 1977.

Kilfeather, Sean, *Vintage Carbery*, Beaver Row Press, Dublin, 1984.

King, Seamus J., *A History of Hurling*, Gill & Macmillan, Dublin, 1998.

Liffey Gaels, *A Century of Gaelic Games, 1884-1984*, Dublin, 1984.

Mahon, Jack, *A History of Gaelic Football*, Gill & Macmillan, Dublin, 2000.

Mandle, W.F. *The GAA and Irish Nationalist Politics, 1884-1924*, Gill & Macmillan, Dublin, 1987.

O'Ceallaigh, Seamus, *Gaelic Days*, Gaelic Athletic Publications, Limerick, 1944.

O'Ceallaigh, Seamus, *Gaelic Athletic Memories*, Gaelic Athletic Publications, Dublin, 1945.

O'Ceallaigh, Seamus, *Story of the GAA*, Wellbrook Press, Freshford, 1977.

O'Hehir, Brendan, *Over the Bar: a personal relationship with the GAA*, Ward River Press, Dublin, 1984.

O'Meára, Micheál (Ed.), *Bloody Sunday; 1920-1995*, Tipperary County Board, Thurles, 1995.

Roscomáin: the Champions, The Park Side Press, Dublin, 1945.

Vaughan, Joseph D., *A Century of Gaelic Games, 1884-1984*, Liffey Gaels, Dublin, 1984.

OTHER

Blát, booklet commemorating the opening of the Hogan Stand, GAA, Dublin, 1959.

British Military Inquiry into Bloody Sunday, Croke Park, 21 November 1920, War Office (WO) 35/88, Public Record Office, Kew, London, England.

Cumann Lúthchleas Gael, Official Records, 1951.

Handbill, ILB 300 p3, National Library of Ireland.

Match Programmes, GAA Museum, Croke Park.

Report of the Commission on the GAA, CLG, Dublin, 1 December 1971.

Index

Page numbers in **bold** indicate pages with photographs. Page numbers with 'c' preceding them indicate photographs in the colour section.